Relationship Conflict Resolution

Achieve Trust and Intimacy Without Endless Arguments - Even If You Feel Stuck in a Cycle of Conflict

Evelyn A. Stonebridge

Heppe-Smith Publishing

Copyright © 2024 by Evelyn A. Stonebridge

All rights reserved.

No portion of this book may be reproduced in any form without written permission from the publisher or author, except as permitted by U.S. copyright law.

This publication is designed to provide accurate and authoritative information in regard to the subject matter covered. It is sold with the understanding that neither the author nor the publisher is engaged in rendering legal, investment, accounting or other professional services. While the publisher and author have used their best efforts in preparing this book, they make no representations or warranties with respect to the accuracy or completeness of the contents of this book and specifically disclaim any implied warranties of merchantability or fitness for a particular purpose. No warranty may be created or extended by sales representatives or written sales materials. The advice and strategies contained herein may not be suitable for your situation. You should consult with a professional when appropriate. Neither the publisher nor the author shall be liable for any loss of profit or any other commercial damages, including but not limited to special, incidental, consequential, personal, or other damages.

Cover Artwork by Getcovers.com

Contents

Introduction	1
1. The Psychology Behind Conflicts	3
2. Communication Breakdowns Unraveled	13
3. Building a Foundation of Effective Communication	28
4. Emotional Intelligence and Regulation	40
5. Conflict Resolution Frameworks	51
6. Rebuilding Trust and Intimacy	65
7. Leveraging Conflict for Personal and Relational Growth	76
8. Inclusive Perspectives on Conflict Resolution	90
9. Addressing Specific Conflicts	103
Conclusion	114
Endnotes	117
About the author	122
Also by	124

Introduction

Conflict is often viewed in every relationship as a looming shadow, a sign that something is amiss. But what if we reframe our perspective? What if we see these conflicts not as roadblocks but as bridges—opportunities to forge deeper connections and understanding between us and our partners? This book embarks on such a transformative journey, acknowledging the challenges and discomfort of conflicts while illuminating their potential to enrich and strengthen our relationships.

As someone deeply entrenched in relationship counseling and conflict resolution, I've witnessed firsthand the power of effective communication, empathy, and understanding in transforming relationships. Working with countless couples and individuals has been my profession and passion. It's driven by a firm belief in the transformative potential of addressing conflicts with the right mindset, tools, and strategies. The insights and approaches shared in this book are a distillation of years of experience, research, and real-life successes in turning relationship challenges into avenues for growth and deeper intimacy.

The purpose of this book is clear: to arm you with the knowledge, strategies, and skills necessary to navigate the sometimes turbulent waters of relationship conflicts. It's designed to be your compass, guiding you towards enhanced communication and rebuilding trust and a deeper connection with your partner. The book offers a comprehensive and relatable guide to understanding and resolving conflicts to benefit you and your partner, fostering personal and relational growth through a blend of the latest research, diverse perspectives, and practical, real-life examples.

This book speaks to a broad audience, from couples in the nascent stages of their relationship to those who have weathered decades together and individuals seeking to improve their ability to communicate and resolve conflicts more effectively. It is crafted to be an invaluable resource for anyone committed to the challenging but rewarding work of building more fulfilling, resilient relationships.

I understand the frustration, the confusion, and the longing that can come with relationship conflicts. I've been there, both personally and professionally. This book invites you to move beyond those feelings to harness the opportunities conflict presents for growth and deeper connection. Through its pages, you will find not just theories but practical, actionable advice and exercises designed to transform your approach to conflicts and, by extension, your relationships.

Let me share a brief story that encapsulates the transformative power of the approaches discussed in this book. A couple I worked with, on the brink of separation, learned to see their recurring arguments not as indicators of their incompatibility but as signals of underlying needs and fears that were not being addressed. By applying the strategies outlined in this book, they resolved their conflicts and discovered a deeper love and respect for each other. Their journey is a testament to the possible positive change when approaching conflicts with the right tools and mindset.

As we journey through this book, I invite you to read and actively engage with the content. Every chapter, exercise, and piece of advice is a step toward resolving conflicts and transforming your relationship into a source of strength, joy, and profound connection.

In the end, the message of this book is simple yet profound: Conflict, when approached with empathy, understanding, and the right strategies, can be the catalyst for incredible growth, deeper understanding, and a closer connection in your relationships. Let's embark on this journey together, turning today's challenges into tomorrow's strengths.

Chapter One

The Psychology Behind Conflicts

> "The quality of our lives depends not on whether or not we have conflicts, but on how we respond to them"
>
> Thomas Crum

The Impact of Stress on Relationship Dynamics

Have you ever noticed how a minor disagreement can suddenly turn into a full-blown argument? It's like watching a tiny spark turn into a raging fire. This phenomenon isn't random; it's deeply rooted in the psychology of stress and its impact on our relationship dynamics. Stress acts like a magnifying glass, making minor irritations appear much more significant than they are, exacerbating tensions, and leading to conflicts that might seem disproportionate to the original issue.

External pressures are often the hidden culprits behind this escalation. Work demands, financial strains, and even social obligations can spill over into our home life, unwittingly increasing the likelihood of conflicts with our partners. When we're under stress, our capacity to handle minor irritations diminishes significantly. What would typically be a small bump in the road becomes a mountain simply because our emotional bandwidth is already stretched thin by external pressures.

Moreover, stress triggers our body's fight or flight response, a primal reaction that isn't always suited to modern relationship dynamics. This response can lead to defensive communication styles, where we're more likely to snap, criticize, or withdraw rather than listen, understand, and empathize. Recognizing this can be a game-changer in how we handle conflicts. When we're stressed, we're not just struggling with the issue at hand but also with an innate physiological response that primes us for conflict rather than resolution.

Identifying when stress is the real culprit behind a conflict is crucial for diffusing tensions. This requires self-awareness and communication that can be challenging to achieve in the heat of the moment. However, strategies such as taking a time-out to cool off, practicing mindfulness to reduce stress levels, and discussing the underlying stressors outside the context of conflict can significantly help. It's about creating a space where both partners can recognize the impact of external stressors and address them without letting them hijack their relationship dynamics.

Understanding the psychology behind conflicts, particularly the role of stress, offers a pathway to healthier, more resilient relationships. By acknowledging and addressing the root causes of our reactions, we can navigate conflicts with greater compassion and understanding, reducing the likelihood of minor irritations escalating into major conflicts.

Emotional Baggage: Unpacking Historical Grievances

It's not just the present that shapes our relationships; the past holds a significant influence, too. Past hurts and unresolved issues often linger, shaping how partners perceive and react to current conflicts. This phenomenon is akin to carrying an invisible backpack filled with all our past emotional injuries, misunderstandings, and heartaches. This 'emotional baggage' can heavily influence our reactions and interactions with our partner, often in ways we're unaware of.

Our early childhood experiences and past relationships are significant contributors to this baggage. They form the lens through which we view our current relationships, affecting our trust levels, communication styles, and self-esteem. For example, someone who experienced abandonment in their past may be hypersensitive to signs of disengagement from their partner, interpreting them as a precursor to abandonment, even if that's not the case.

The concept of projection plays a critical role here. It's too easy to project our fears, insecurities, and unresolved issues onto our partner, leading to misinterpretations of their actions or words. This misalignment can create a breeding ground for conflict, as reactions are based on past experiences rather than the present reality.

Navigating this requires a deliberate effort to separate past experiences from present interactions. This involves recognizing when our reactions are disproportionate to the current situation, indicating that past baggage is at play. Communication is critical in these moments. Sharing our triggers and vulnerabilities with our partners can help them better understand our reactions and create a supportive environment for unpacking this emotional baggage.

Moreover, mindfulness and therapy can be invaluable in this journey, offering tools to process past hurts and develop healthier emotional responses. By consciously separating past experiences from present interactions, we can reduce unnecessary conflict escalation and build a more understanding, empathetic connection with our partner.

While our past shapes us, it doesn't have to define our present relationships. Acknowledging and working through our emotional baggage can lay the groundwork for healthier, more fulfilling partnerships.

Attachment Styles and Their Role in Conflict

Our approach to conflicts in relationships is deeply influenced by our attachment style, a framework of emotional bonding formed in early childhood. Understanding these styles can be a key to navigating relationship dynamics more effectively.

There are four primary attachment styles: **secure, anxious-preoccupied, dismissive-avoidant, and fearful-avoidant**. Each style has its own characteristics that influence how we interact with our partners. Securely attached individuals tend to handle conflict constructively, communicating openly and empathetically. Anxious-preoccupied individuals may seek more reassurance and struggle with fears of abandonment. Dismissive-avoidant individuals often distance themselves in conflicts, valuing independence over connection. Fearful-avoidant individuals face a tug-of-war between desiring closeness and fearing it, leading to mixed signals during conflicts.

Mismatched attachment styles between partners can lead to recurring conflicts due to differing needs and communication methods. For instance, an anxious-preoccupied individual paired with a dismissive-avoidant partner may find themselves in a cycle of pursuing and withdrawing, respectively.

Recognizing one's attachment style is the first step towards managing conflict more effectively. This self-awareness allows us to understand our reactions and needs within the relationship better. Adapting communication strategies to address these needs constructively can help mitigate conflicts. For example, securely attached individuals can reassure anxious-preoccupied partners, while those with avoidant styles might work on opening up more to foster a deeper connection.

> Attachment styles, developed early in life, significantly influence how we form and maintain relationships. Recognizing your attachment style can help you understand personal relationship patterns, including how you handle closeness, emotional intimacy, and conflict. Here's a brief overview to help you identify your attachment style:
> - **Secure Attachment**: Individuals feel comfortable with intimacy and independence in relationships. They're often empathetic, understanding, and good at communicating their needs and responding to their partner's needs.
>
> - **Anxious-Preoccupied Attachment**: These individuals seek high levels of intimacy, approval, and reassurance but may feel anxious about their partner's ability to provide them. They often fear abandonment.
>
> - **Dismissive-Avoidant Attachment**: People with this style prefer independence to intimacy, often distancing themselves emotionally from their partner. They may prioritize self-sufficiency and downplay the importance of relationships.
>
> - **Fearful-Avoidant Attachment** (also known as disorganized): Individuals have mixed feelings about close relationships, craving emotional closeness but fearing trust and reliance on others due to past traumas or rejections.

> Identifying your attachment style is a step toward healthier relationships, allowing for greater self-awareness and understanding of how you interact with others.

Understanding and adapting to our and our partner's attachment styles can create a more harmonious and supportive relationship environment, even in the face of conflicts.

The Influence of Personality Traits on Conflict Resolution

Personality traits profoundly impact how we navigate and resolve conflicts. The Big Five personality traits—openness, conscientiousness, extraversion, agreeableness, and neuroticism—offer a comprehensive framework to understand these dynamics.

- **Openness**: People who score high in the personality trait of openness tend to tackle conflicts with a sense of creativity and curiosity. They are more likely to approach such situations with an open mind, keeping their options open and searching for innovative and out-of-the-box solutions that others may not have considered. This tendency to embrace novel ideas and approaches often enables them to find new and effective ways to resolve conflicts that others may have overlooked or dismissed.

- **Conscientiousness**: Individuals who exhibit high levels of conscientiousness tend to approach conflicts in a thorough and systematic manner, with a strong emphasis on achieving outcomes that are just and structured. They are generally diligent and meticulous in their problem-solving approach, taking the time to carefully consider all relevant factors and perspectives before making any decisions. These individuals are highly motivated to maintain fairness and order in their interactions with others, and will often go to great lengths to ensure that everyone involved in a conflict is treated equitably and with respect. Overall, their conscientious nature makes them effective mediators and problem solvers in a wide range of settings.

- **Extraversion**: Individuals who possess an extraverted personality type tend to have a more direct and assertive approach towards conflict resolution. They usually prefer to address the issues at hand openly and are not afraid to speak their minds. They tend to be outgoing and sociable in nature, which makes them comfortable with discussing problems with others. Due to their outgoing nature, they may come across as more confident and bold, and may not shy away from expressing their opinions and thoughts in a straightforward manner. This approach can be effective in resolving conflicts quickly and efficiently.

- **Agreeableness**: Individuals who display high levels of agreeableness tend to prioritize maintaining a peaceful and harmonious environment in their social interactions. They are more likely to consider the needs and feelings of others and are willing to compromise or defer to them during conflicts, even if it means sacrificing some of their own personal desires. This trait is associated with a cooperative, empathetic, and compassionate nature, which makes them more approachable and likable by others.

- **Neuroticism**: Neuroticism is a personality trait that refers to the tendency of an individual to experience negative emotions such as anxiety, fear, and emotional instability. People with high neuroticism levels may find it difficult to handle conflicts as they tend to feel more anxious and emotionally overwhelmed during such situations. This can have an impact on their ability to come up with effective conflict resolution strategies. They may struggle to think rationally and may react impulsively, leading to further complications. Therefore, it is important to understand how neuroticism affects conflict resolution strategies and to develop strategies that can help individuals overcome these challenges.

Effective conflict resolution is a crucial aspect of maintaining healthy relationships. One of the key factors that can influence the success of conflict resolution is the compatibility of personalities. Personality compatibility refers to how well two individuals' personalities mesh together in terms of their traits, values, and attitudes. When partners have complementary personality traits, such as one being high in agreeableness and the other in conscientiousness, it can significantly enhance their ability to resolve conflicts in a positive manner.

Complementary traits enable partners to leverage their differences to find constructive solutions to conflicts. For example, when one partner is more agreeable and the other is more conscientious, they can use these traits to their advantage by acknowledging each other's strengths and adopting a flexible approach to problem-solving. This means that they can work together to find a middle ground that takes into account both of their perspectives.

To foster a more constructive and empathetic approach to resolving conflicts, individuals must first understand and respect these personality differences. By recognizing that everyone has unique personality traits and values, they can begin to appreciate the strengths and weaknesses that each partner brings to the table. This can help them to approach conflicts with a more open-minded and empathetic mindset, which can lead to more positive outcomes.

Mindsets: Fixed vs. Growth in Conflict Scenarios

The mindset we adopt in the face of conflicts plays a pivotal role in their outcomes. Understanding the distinction between a fixed and a growth mindset can illuminate why some conflicts escalate while others lead to stronger bonds.

Individuals with a **fixed mindset** perceive their capabilities and skills as static and unchangeable. They tend to avoid conflicts or engage in them with the sole objective of 'winning', even if it means compromising the health of their relationships. This perspective can create a significant barrier to open communication and empathy, as admitting fault or seeking a compromise may feel like an admission of weakness or defeat. Consequently, individuals with a fixed mindset may struggle to build positive and meaningful relationships, as they may prioritize their ego and personal interests over the needs and feelings of others.

In contrast to a fixed mindset, which tends to view challenges and conflicts as threats and obstacles to be avoided, a **growth mindset** approaches such situations with a different perspective. Rather than fearing or avoiding conflict, it embraces it as an opportunity for growth and learning. This mindset encourages individuals to be open-minded, curious, and willing to engage in dialogue with others, even when they hold different perspectives or opinions. Rather than trying to "win" or dominate the conversation, those with a growth mindset seek to understand the other person's point of view and work together toward resolution. By doing so, they not only strengthen their relationships but also learn valuable skills in communication, empathy, and conflict resolution. Ultimately, the growth mindset sees conflicts as a chance to deepen mutual understanding, build trust, and foster personal and professional development.

Cultivating a Growth Mindset in Conflict Resolution

Embrace Challenges as Opportunities for Growth
Viewing conflicts as opportunities rather than threats can significantly alter their outcomes. This mindset encourages individuals to approach disagreements with curiosity and openness, seeking to understand and learn from the root causes. Rather than avoiding difficult conversations, see them as a chance to deepen understanding and connection with your partner. This approach fosters resilience and adaptability, critical components of a strong relationship.

Practice Active Listening and Empathy
Active listening involves fully concentrating, understanding, responding, and remembering what is being said. In conflicts, it means putting aside one's agenda to hear and empathize with your partner's perspective truly. This practice can bridge gaps in understanding and build mutual respect, making it easier to find common ground. Empathy allows us to connect with our partner's emotions, making them feel valued and understood, which is crucial for resolving conflicts constructively.

Focus on Solutions that Benefit the Relationship
Instead of aiming to 'win' the argument, aim to find solutions that strengthen the relationship. This involves looking for compromises or creative solutions that address both partners' needs and concerns. By prioritizing the health and well-being of the relationship over individual victories, you foster an environment where both partners feel supported and valued. This collaborative approach not only resolves the immediate conflict but also builds a foundation for more effective communication in the future.

Reflect on Conflicts as Learning Experiences
Every conflict offers valuable lessons about ourselves, our partners, and our relationship dynamics. Taking time to reflect on these situations can provide insights into how to handle similar issues in the future better. Discussing what worked, what didn't, and how each partner felt during the process can be incredibly enlightening. This reflection fosters a culture of continuous improvement and personal growth, ensuring that both partners evolve together through their challenges.

Adopting these practices can transform how conflicts are perceived and handled, turning potential sources of friction into opportunities for strengthening the bond between partners.

Conclusion

In this chapter, we explored the profound impact of psychological elements like stress, emotional baggage, attachment styles, personality traits, and mindsets on conflict resolution within relationships. Each section offered insights into why conflicts arise and provided strategies for constructively navigating these challenges.

- **Stress** magnifies minor irritations, turning them into significant conflicts, emphasizing the importance of recognizing and managing stress in our relationships.

- **Emotional Baggage** reminded us how past experiences shape our reactions in the present, urging us to differentiate between past hurts and current issues.

- Through **Attachment Styles**, we saw how early childhood experiences influence our approach to conflict, highlighting the importance of understanding and adapting to our and our partner's attachment styles.

- The discussion on **Personality Traits** shed light on how the Big Five personality traits affect our conflict styles, advocating for leveraging complementary traits to enhance conflict resolution.

- Finally, **Mindsets** showed us that approaching conflicts with a growth mindset can transform them into opportunities for strengthening relationships.

Looking ahead to Chapter 2, "Communication Breakdowns Unraveled," we'll delve into the nuances of communication—its breakdowns, barriers, and its pivotal role in either exacerbating conflicts or facilitating resolution. This next chapter will provide practical tips and strategies to improve communication skills, ensuring you and your partner can navigate misunderstandings and maintain a healthy, fulfilling relationship.

As we continue our exploration into communication, remember the wisdom of Kenneth Kaye: "If we manage conflict constructively, we harness its energy for creativity and development," reminding us of the transformative power of effectively navigating conflicts.

Chapter Two

Communication Breakdowns Unraveled

"The single biggest problem in communication is the illusion that it has taken place."

George Bernard Shaw

The Art of Active Listening and its Missteps

Active listening is a cornerstone of effective communication, especially in intimate relationships. It's more than just hearing your partner's words; it's about engaging fully and understanding their perspective without interfering with your own biases or preconceptions. Let's dive into the critical components of active listening and identify common missteps that can hinder communication.

Critical Components of Active Listening

Active listening is an essential skill that requires giving your full attention to your partner. It means putting aside any distractions such as phones, other activities, or thoughts, and focusing entirely on your partner's words, tone of voice, and non-verbal cues. When you are actively listening, you are present in the moment and showing your partner that they are your priority.

Reflective feedback is the final component of active listening. After listening, reflecting back on what you have heard is important to show understanding. This can involve paraphrasing your partner's words or summarizing their main points. Reflective feedback helps clarify misunderstandings and validates your partner's feelings and experiences. It shows your partner that you have been actively listening and that you understand what they are trying to communicate.

Withholding judgment is another crucial aspect of active listening. It means listening without jumping to conclusions or judging your partner's words and actions. This openness allows your partner to express themselves freely, fostering a safe and trusting environment. Withholding judgment means putting aside your reactions and viewpoints to understand theirs truly, even if you don't agree with them.

Common Pitfalls

One common mistake many people make while listening is interrupting their partner while they are speaking. This can be disruptive to their train of thought and can signal that your response is more important than what they are saying, which can be invalidating. Interrupting can lead to miscommunication and misunderstandings, which can harm your relationship with your partner. When you interrupt, you may miss important details or nuances in their message, which can result in misinterpretation. Moreover, interrupting can make your partner feel unheard, disrespected, and disregarded. Therefore, it is essential to practice active listening skills, which include paying attention, clarifying, and summarizing what your partner is saying. Active listening also involves being present in the moment, showing empathy, and giving your partner the space to express themselves fully.

So, the next time you find yourself tempted to interrupt your partner, take a deep breath, and remind yourself that your response can wait. Instead, focus on understanding their perspective, ask questions to clarify their points, and give them the chance to finish their thought. By doing so, you will demonstrate that you value their opinion, build trust, and strengthen your relationship.

One of the most common communication pitfalls is the tendency to plan your response instead of actively listening to your conversation partner. When you're preoccupied with formulating your next comment or rebuttal, you may miss important nuances in the other person's message. This lack of attentiveness can lead to misunderstandings, hurt feelings, and missed opportunities for genuine connection. Instead, try to focus on what the other person is saying without immediately jumping to your own conclusions. Take the time to reflect on their perspective and consider how you can respond in a way that promotes understanding and facilitates productive dialogue. By prioritizing active listening, you can build stronger relationships and avoid unnecessary conflict.

Exercises to Develop Active Listening

1. **Reflective Listening Exercise**: Take turns sharing thoughts or feelings with your partner. The listener should focus solely on understanding and reflecting back what was said without offering advice or opinions. This practice helps hone your ability to provide reflective feedback and deeply understand your partner's perspective.

2. **Non-Verbal Cues Exercise**: Engage in a conversation where you pay close attention to non-verbal cues, such as body language, facial expressions, and tone of voice. After the conversation, share what you observed and how it added context to spoken words. This exercise enhances your ability to read and respond to non-verbal communication effectively.

3. **Distraction-Free Conversations**: Set aside time for conversations where all potential distractions, such as phones and computers, are removed. Focus on giving each other your full attention and practicing listening without interrupting or judging. This setting can reinforce the habit of full engagement in your daily interactions.

By understanding and practicing the art of active listening, couples can navigate misunderstandings more effectively and build a stronger, more empathetic connection. Remember, communication is about conveying your thoughts and being a receptive and understanding listener to your partner's needs and feelings.

Misinterpretations and Assumptions: The Silent Relationship Killers

Relationships are complex and require constant maintenance. However, even with the best intentions, misunderstandings and assumptions can creep in and damage the relationship from the inside out. These silent killers can cause significant harm before the problem is recognized, leading to arguments, conflicts, and even breakups.

Misinterpretations arise when one or both partners fail to understand each other's feelings, emotions, or intentions. This can happen because of a lack of communication, a failure to listen actively, or simply a difference in perception.

Assumptions, on the other hand, occur when one partner makes a judgment based on incomplete information or a preconceived notion. This can lead to misunderstandings and unnecessary conflicts that could have been avoided with better communication.

Over time, these misunderstandings and assumptions can erode the trust and intimacy that is essential to a healthy relationship. That's why it is crucial to address them promptly and openly, with honesty, patience, and empathy. By doing so, couples can strengthen their bond, deepen their understanding of each other, and build a relationship that will last a lifetime.

Lack of Clarity Leads to Assumptions: In any communication, the lack of clarity can cause misunderstandings and lead to assumptions. When we are unable to understand our partner's intentions clearly, we tend to fill in the gaps with our own interpretations, which may not be accurate. This misinterpretation is particularly dangerous because it creates a reaction based on a situation that we have misunderstood or distorted due to our perceptions, rather than what was actually communicated. It can lead to confusion, frustration, and even conflict, which could have been avoided if we had taken the time to clarify and understand the message. Therefore, it is crucial to ensure that our communication is clear, concise, and unambiguous to avoid any misinterpretation and assumptions.

The Role of Cognitive Biases: The way we process information is not always entirely objective. Our cognitive biases tend to play a significant role in shaping how we interpret the words and actions of those around us. These biases are essentially shortcuts that our brain takes to simplify the information processing, but they can end up distorting our understanding of others' intentions. One of the most common cognitive biases is confirmation bias. This bias leads us to pay more attention to information that confirms our pre-existing beliefs or assumptions.

In the context of relationships, these biases can have a profound impact. For example, if we have a belief that our partner is neglectful, we are more likely to interpret their actions as further evidence of this, regardless of their actual intentions. This can lead to misunderstandings and conflicts, causing further damage to the relationship. It is essential to be aware of these biases and work towards overcoming them to foster healthy and transparent communication in relationships.

Strategies for Clarification and Verification:

1. **Ask for Clarification**: Instead of assuming you understand what your partner means, ask them to clarify. Phrases like "Can you help me understand what you mean by that?" or "Did you mean..." can open the door to more transparent communication.

2. **Repeat Back What You Heard**: This strategy involves repeating what you think your partner said in your own words. It allows them to correct any misinterpretations and ensures you're both on the same page.

3. **Avoid Jumping to Conclusions**: Take a moment to reflect before reacting. Consider whether your response is based on facts or assumptions. If you need more clarification about your partner's intentions, it's always better to ask than to assume.

4. **Practice Mindfulness in Communication**: Being present in your conversations helps you focus on what is being said rather than what you expect to hear. This presence can reduce the likelihood of misinterpretations.

By actively working to clarify and verify information before reacting, couples can prevent many unnecessary conflicts. Open, clear communication is essential in nurturing a healthy, understanding, and assumption-free relationship. Remember, it's not just about avoiding misinterpretations but actively building a foundation of trust and clarity that supports the growth and depth of the relationship.

Non-Verbal Cues: What We Say Without Words

Non-verbal communication is an essential aspect of building and maintaining relationships. It refers to the use of body language, facial expressions, and tone of voice, among other cues, to convey messages and emotions. These non-verbal signals can be more potent than spoken words and can significantly impact how our partners perceive and interpret our communication. By paying attention to non-verbal cues, we can enhance the effectiveness of our communication and strengthen our relationships.

Forms of Non-Verbal Communication:

- **Body Language**: The way we carry ourselves and move in our environment can reveal a great deal about our thoughts and feelings. For example, crossing our arms in front of our chest might indicate a sense of defensiveness or discomfort. Conversely, leaning forward and making eye contact can signify attentiveness, interest, and engagement in the conversation or activity taking place. Other non-verbal cues such as facial expressions, tone of voice, and body language can also provide valuable insights into our emotional state and intentions. By paying attention to these subtle signals, we can gain a deeper understanding of ourselves and others, and communicate more effectively in a variety of social and professional settings.

- **Tone of Voice**: The words we choose to express ourselves are just one part of effective communication. Equally important is the way we deliver those words. The tone we use, whether it's sarcastic, gentle, direct, or something else entirely, can drastically affect how our message is received. For instance, a sarcastic tone can add a layer of irony or humor to a sentence, but it can also change the intended meaning of the words. On the other hand, a gentle tone can soften a message that might otherwise come across as harsh or critical. Therefore, it's essential to pay attention to the tone we use when communicating, as it can make all the difference in how our message is perceived and understood.

- **Facial Expressions**: Facial expressions are a powerful means of communication that can often convey emotions more accurately than words. The human face is capable of conveying a wide range of emotions, from joy and excitement to sadness and disapproval, and everything in between. A genuine smile, for instance, can ease tension and create a positive atmosphere, while a frown can indicate disapproval, frustration, or sadness. Other facial expressions, such as raised eyebrows, squinted eyes, or a tilted head, can also provide important cues about a person's emotional state, thoughts, or intentions. Overall, paying attention to facial expressions can be a valuable tool in understanding and connecting with others.

Impact of Non-Verbal Cues:
Positive non-verbal cues, such as nodding or smiling, can significantly enhance the warmth and clarity of a message, making the receiver feel understood and appreciated. Conversely, negative cues like rolling eyes or a dismissive hand gesture can escalate a conflict, regardless of the spoken words.

Tips for Awareness and Interpretation:

1. **Self-Awareness**: Non-verbal communication plays a vital role in our daily interactions. To improve your communication skills, it's important to pay attention to your non-verbal signals, such as your gestures, facial expressions, and tone of voice. One way to become more aware of your non-verbal cues is by recording yourself during a conversation and observing your behavior. This can help you understand how others may perceive your non-verbal signals and how they may impact your message.

When reviewing the recording, pay attention to your eye contact, posture, and hand gestures. Are you making enough eye contact, or are you looking away too often? Is your posture open and inviting, or closed and defensive? Are your hand gestures too frequent or distracting? Additionally, observe your facial expressions and tone of voice. Do you appear engaged and interested in the conversation, or bored and disinterested? Is your tone of voice confident and assertive, or hesitant and uncertain?

2. **Mindful Observation**: In order to have a successful and healthy conversation with your partner, it's crucial to pay close attention to their non-verbal cues. Non-verbal cues can often be more informative than verbal communication, as they can reveal a person's true feelings and emotions. Examples of non-verbal cues

include body language, facial expressions, and tone of voice.

It's important to observe whether your partner's non-verbal cues align with what they are saying verbally. For instance, if your partner is saying "I'm fine" but their tone of voice is flat and their arms are crossed, it may indicate that they are not actually fine. Similarly, if they are nodding but their facial expression is tense, it may suggest that they are not fully agreeing with what you're saying.

3. **Clarification**: In case you find yourself unsure about what your partner is trying to convey through their non-verbal cues, it's always a good idea to ask for clarification. Instead of making assumptions, it's best to initiate a dialogue by acknowledging their body language and expressing your concern in a non-confrontational manner. For instance, you could say something like "I noticed that you seemed a bit tense just now. Is everything okay? Would you like to talk about it?" This kind of approach can help prevent misunderstandings, build trust, and foster healthy communication in your relationship.

4. **Practice Empathy**: When communicating with your partner, it's important to pay attention to their non-verbal cues such as their body language, tone of voice, and facial expressions. These cues can often reveal the underlying emotions that they may not be expressing verbally. By trying to understand these emotions from your partner's perspective, you can develop empathy towards their feelings, which can in turn help you respond more effectively and compassionately. Empathy involves acknowledging and accepting your partner's emotions without judgment, and can help you build a stronger emotional connection with them. So, the next time you're communicating with your partner, try to put yourself in their shoes and understand their non-verbal cues to respond with empathy and compassion.

In order to effectively communicate in a relationship, it is important to be aware of and understand the non-verbal cues that are being conveyed. These cues can include body language, facial expressions, tone of voice, and other subtle indicators that are not necessarily articulated through words. By becoming more attuned to these non-verbal cues, individuals can gain a deeper understanding of their partner's emotions, thoughts, and intentions, which can ultimately lead to a stronger connection.

Recognizing and respecting these silent messages is crucial for building and maintaining healthy relationships. Misinterpretation of non-verbal cues can lead to misunderstandings, hurt feelings, and conflict. By paying attention to these cues and responding appropriately, individuals can enhance their communication, reduce misunderstandings, and strengthen their bonds without ever saying a word.

Some common non-verbal cues that can be important to recognize in a relationship include posture, eye contact, facial expressions, tone of voice, and gestures. For example, crossed arms or a furrowed brow may indicate defensiveness or disagreement, while a smile or open posture may signal agreement or interest. It is also important to consider cultural differences in non-verbal communication, as different cultures may have different norms and expectations for how non-verbal cues are interpreted.

Overall, developing a heightened awareness of non-verbal cues and treating them with respect and attention can be an effective way to enhance communication and build stronger relationships.

The Dangers of Digital Miscommunication in Relationships

In today's world, where technology has taken over almost every aspect of our lives, communication has become more efficient, fast, and convenient than ever before. However, with the rise of digital communication methods like text messages, emails, and instant messaging services, there are a few challenges and risks that we need to be aware of, especially when it comes to our personal relationships.

One of the most significant challenges with digital communication is that it can lead to misinterpretations and misunderstandings. Unlike face-to-face communication, digital communication lacks tone of voice, facial expressions, and body language, which can lead to miscommunication. For instance, an innocent message can be perceived as sarcastic or rude, causing unnecessary conflicts and misunderstandings between people.

Moreover, digital communication can also promote a sense of detachment and impersonality, which can strain relationships. When we communicate digitally, we tend to focus more on the message content and less on the emotional context, which can make us appear cold, distant, and uninterested. This can lead to feelings of neglect and dissatisfaction in our relationships, especially if one person feels like they are always the one initiating the conversation.

Therefore, it is important to be aware of the potential risks of digital communication and take steps to overcome them. This can include being mindful of our tone and language, using emojis or visual cues to convey emotions, and making an effort to have face-to-face conversations whenever possible. By doing so, we can strengthen our relationships and ensure that our digital communication is helping us connect with others, rather than causing unnecessary stress and misunderstandings.

Lack of Non-Verbal Cues:
Digital communication has become an integral part of our lives, but it comes with its own set of challenges. One of the most significant issues is the lack of non-verbal cues. When we communicate face-to-face, we rely on body language, facial expressions, and tone of voice to understand the meaning and emotion behind a message. However, in text-based communication, these cues are absent, making it easy to misinterpret the intent or emotion behind a message. A joke can be taken as an offense, and genuine concern can be mistaken for criticism. This often leads to misunderstandings and conflicts, which could have been easily avoided if we had the benefit of non-verbal cues.

Textual Tone Misinterpretation:
In today's digital age, people communicate with others through written communication more often than ever before. While this can be convenient and efficient, it can also present some challenges. One of the main challenges is the phenomenon of 'textual tone', which refers to the emotional tone that we infer from digital messages. However, despite our best efforts, it can often be easy to get it wrong.

In written communication, we don't have the benefit of seeing a person's facial expressions or hearing the tone of their voice. This makes it difficult to accurately gauge the emotional content of a message. For instance, a short reply may be interpreted as disinterest or anger when, in reality, the sender might simply be busy or distracted. This misinterpretation of tone can lead to unnecessary conflicts and hurt feelings, as individuals react not to the intended message but to their perception of it.

Therefore, it's important to be mindful of how our messages may be perceived by the recipient. We can use emoticons, capitalization, and punctuation to help convey the intended tone of our messages. Additionally, it's important to give the benefit of the doubt and not assume negative intent when receiving a message that may seem ambiguous or curt. By being mindful of textual tone and taking steps to clarify our messages, we can avoid misunderstandings and promote clear, effective communication.

Choosing Face-to-Face Communication:
To mitigate the risks of digital miscommunication, it's crucial to know when to choose face-to-face communication over digital methods. Here are a few guidelines:

- **Sensitive Topics**: When it comes to discussing sensitive topics or matters that are likely to provoke strong emotions, it is always preferable to have the conversation in person. This approach enables the parties involved to quickly clarify any misunderstandings and ensure that everyone has a clear understanding of the situation. Engaging in face-to-face communication can also help to establish a sense of trust and mutual respect, leading to a more productive and positive outcome.

- **Misunderstandings Arise**: When communicating with someone via digital means, it's not uncommon for misunderstandings to arise due to the lack of nonverbal cues and context. In such situations, it can be helpful to switch to a phone call or an in-person conversation to clarify things more effectively. By doing so, you can ensure that both parties are on the same page and avoid any further confusion or misinterpretation.

- **Complex Conversations**: When it comes to conversations that demand a keen understanding of subtleties and complexities, nothing beats face-to-face communication. This mode of communication provides the opportunity for a more thorough and complete exchange of ideas, opinions and feelings. It enables individuals to express themselves more fully, allowing for a deeper level of engagement and a more meaningful connection.

By being mindful of the limitations of digital communication and choosing the appropriate medium for our messages, we can reduce the risk of miscommunication and maintain healthier relationships. Remember, sometimes a quick call or a face-to-face chat can do wonders for clarity and understanding, keeping our connections strong and misunderstandings at bay.

Escalation: When Small Disagreements Turn into Big Battles

In any relationship, it is vital to understand the dynamics of escalation in conflicts to ensure a healthy and fulfilling bond with your partner. Even a minor disagreement can quickly escalate into a significant battle, causing long-term damage to the relationship. Therefore, it is essential to recognize common triggers that cause conflicts and learn effective de-escalation techniques to prevent minor disputes from escalating.

De-escalation techniques can be helpful in managing conflicts. Active listening is one such technique where you listen attentively to the other person's perspective and acknowledge their feelings without interrupting or invalidating them. By taking a break, both parties can cool down and regroup before continuing the conversation. Using "I" statements can help in expressing your feelings without making accusations or blaming the other person. Finding common ground is another effective technique that involves identifying shared interests or goals to help both parties reach a mutually beneficial solution.

Recognizing common triggers is also crucial in preventing conflicts from escalating. These can include differences in opinion, misunderstandings, unmet expectations, and emotional outbursts. By identifying these triggers and addressing them, couples can prevent minor disagreements from becoming major conflicts.

By using effective de-escalation techniques and recognizing common triggers, couples can foster a healthy relationship built on mutual respect, understanding, and effective communication. It is important to maintain open communication, empathy, and a willingness to compromise to ensure a long-lasting and fulfilling relationship.

Common Triggers of Escalation:

- **Stress and Tiredness**: Humans are susceptible to experiencing irritability when subjected to external pressures such as excessive work stress or lack of proper sleep. This heightened irritability can lead to overreactions even over trivial issues that would otherwise not cause any major concern.

- **Unrelated Frustrations**: At times, we may find ourselves dealing with frustrations that have nothing to do with our partner. However, these frustrations often have the potential to affect the way we interact with our partner. This can cause even a minor disagreement to escalate into a full-blown argument, as we unconsciously use it as an outlet for the unrelated issues we are currently dealing with.

- **Defensive Communication Styles**: When a person perceives a threat or feels attacked in a conversation, they may respond by employing defensive communication tactics. These tactics can take many forms, including counterattacking the other person or withdrawing from the conversation altogether. However, these defensive strategies often serve to escalate the conflict further and can make it more difficult to reach a resolution.

Role of Defensive Communication Styles:
In interpersonal communication, defensive communication styles can have a major impact on the escalation of conflicts. When one partner perceives criticism or attack from the other, their response can either be to immediately defend themselves aggressively, leading to a cycle of attack and defend, or to withdraw and shut down, which can be frustrating for the other partner and potentially escalate the disagreement further. These defensive communication styles are often rooted in a fear of being vulnerable or a desire to protect one's self-esteem, but unfortunately, they can often make conflict resolution more difficult and prolong the disagreement.

De-escalation Techniques and Strategies:

1. **Take a Timeout**: It is advisable to be aware of your emotions during a discussion and take a short pause if you feel they are getting out of control. This can help prevent any impulsive actions or words that may lead to regret later on.

2. **Use "I" Statements**: When expressing our emotions and requirements to someone, it's crucial to do so in a way that doesn't put the blame on them. By doing this, we can ensure that the conversation remains open and non-defensive, allowing both parties to communicate effectively.

3. **Active Listening**: When you find yourself in a heated argument with your partner, it can be tempting to focus only on getting your own point across. However, taking the time to actively listen to your partner's perspective can be incredibly valuable in de-escalating tensions. One technique to help achieve this is to acknowledge their feelings and offer empathy. By doing so, you show your partner that you care about their point of view and are willing to work together to find a resolution that works for both of you. This can help to create a more positive and constructive dialogue, leading to a healthier and happier relationship overall.

4. **Agree to Disagree**: In any relationship, disagreements are bound to happen. However, it's crucial to remember that not every disagreement needs to turn into a full-blown conflict. Sometimes, it's better to agree to disagree on minor issues to prevent the situation from escalating unnecessarily. By choosing our battles wisely, we can prioritize what truly matters and avoid getting bogged down by trivial matters.

5. **Seek to Understand, Not to Win**: When engaging in a disagreement with your partner, it can be more effective to approach the conversation with the intention of understanding their viewpoint, rather than focusing solely on winning the argument. This shift in approach can lead to a change in the overall dynamic of the conversation, fostering more mutual respect and a deeper understanding of each other's perspectives.

In any relationship, disagreements are bound to arise from time to time. However, couples can learn to manage these disagreements constructively by employing specific strategies. This enables them to prevent minor issues from escalating into significant conflicts that could threaten the stability of their relationship. Understanding the underlying triggers and dynamics at play is crucial for partners to intervene effectively before a small disagreement becomes a big battle. By doing so, couples can communicate their thoughts and feelings in a calm and respectful manner, thereby resolving any conflicts that arise in a manner that is beneficial for both parties involved.

Conclusion

Chapter 2, "Communication Breakdowns Unraveled," has meticulously delved into the intricate dynamics of communication within relationships, emphasizing the paramount importance of active listening, recognizing and interpreting non-verbal cues, navigating the treacherous waters of digital communication, and understanding the escalation of conflicts. We explored how misinterpretations, assumptions, and the absence of physical cues in digital exchanges can significantly distort the intended messages, leading to unnecessary misunderstandings and disputes. Practical exercises and strategies have been provided to enhance active listening, interpret non-verbal signals accurately, and choose the most appropriate mode of communication to foster understanding and minimize conflicts.

As we pivot to Chapter 3, "Building a Foundation of Effective Communication," we will explore mastering active listening, expressing needs clearly and compassionately, and utilizing "I" statements to own your feelings. This upcoming chapter aims to solidify the communication skills necessary for thriving relationships, providing actionable steps to enhance empathy, validation, and mutual understanding.

To encapsulate the essence of this chapter and the transition to the next, consider the insight at the start of the chapter: "The single biggest problem in communication is the illusion that it has taken place." - George Bernard Shaw. This quote serves as a powerful reminder of the common pitfalls in communication. It underscores the importance of the strategies and insights provided in Chapter 2 as foundational steps toward more profound relational connections and effective conflict resolution.

Chapter Three

Building a Foundation of Effective Communication

"Most people do not listen with the intent to understand; they listen with the intent to reply."
— Stephen R. Covey

Elevating Understanding Through Active Listening

Effective communication is an integral part of maintaining healthy relationships. It is vital in establishing personal connections and keeping them vibrant over time. The previous chapters discussed the basics of initiating and sustaining a dialogue. In this segment, we will focus on improving our listening skills.

Active listening is not merely hearing what the other person is saying, but it is the art of engaging with their words, emotions, and thoughts. It requires peeling back the layers of conversation to uncover the essence of what is being communicated. Active listening is about paying attention to non-verbal cues, such as body language, tone of voice, facial expressions, and words being spoken.

By actively listening to others, we can understand their perspective and build empathy, essential for maintaining healthy relationships. It allows us to comprehend their emotions and thoughts and respond in an appropriate and helpful way. Active listening is a powerful tool that can help us deepen our connections with others and foster more meaningful relationships.

Enhancing Empathy and Validation: Active listening is a complex skill that requires more than just hearing what someone is saying. It involves immersing oneself in the speaker's perspective, understanding their point of view, and offering emotional support without judgment. It's about creating a safe and comfortable space where the speaker's thoughts and feelings are heard, felt, and respected, regardless of whether you agree with them.

Through active listening, you can demonstrate a higher level of empathy and validation that encourages a deeper, more genuine exchange of ideas and emotions. This can help build trust and rapport between individuals, improve relationships, and foster greater understanding and mutual respect. Active listening can be especially useful when emotions are high, such as during a disagreement or when someone is going through a difficult time.

To become a better active listener, practicing being present in the moment, giving your full attention to the speaker, and avoiding distractions is important. You should also try to understand the speaker's perspective by asking open-ended questions, paraphrasing what they say, and summarizing their main points. Finally, active listening requires patience, empathy, and a willingness to put yourself in the other person's shoes. Doing so can create a more positive and meaningful interaction that benefits both parties.

The Subtleties of Non-Verbal Communication: Our body language can communicate more than we say aloud. The way we nod, smile or lean forward can convey a lot of support and attention. These nonverbal cues can be further reinforced by verbal affirmations such as "I see" or "Go on, I'm listening," which can further emphasize that we are fully present in the conversation. Combining these gestures with active listening skills can build trust and establish a genuine connection with the person we are interacting with. This can help foster more meaningful, effective communication and positive outcomes in personal and professional relationships.

Practical Steps for Active Listening Mastery: We must transform our intentions into actions as we strive to improve our communication skills. One way to achieve this is by incorporating exercises that promote active listening into our daily interactions. We can better understand and respond to others' perspectives by actively listening. One such exercise is paraphrasing, which involves restating the speaker's message in our own words to confirm our understanding. Another exercise is asking open-ended questions, which allow the speaker to elaborate and provide more detail. By practicing these exercises, we create an environment where every voice is valued and understood, and we can foster deeper connections with those around us.

Navigating the Obstacles of Active Listening: Active listening is an essential component of effective communication, which requires us to be fully present and engaged in the conversation. However, various distractions, judgments, and emotional triggers often hinder our ability to listen attentively. These barriers can manifest in multiple ways, such as daydreaming, interrupting, or losing focus on the speaker's message.

To overcome these hurdles, it is crucial to recognize and address them head-on. This involves becoming aware of our biases, prejudices, and preconceptions that may cloud our ability to listen without judgment. By acknowledging these barriers, we can work towards fostering a more empathetic and open-hearted dialogue.

Moreover, being mindful of external distractions such as noise, technology, or other environmental factors can also improve our listening skills. We can create a conducive environment for more meaningful and impactful communication by actively minimizing these disruptions.

Ultimately, by working to clear these hurdles, we pave the way for more effective and satisfying communication, which fosters mutual understanding and respect.

As we journey through the nuances of active listening, we discover that it's not just about enhancing our conversations but enriching our connections. By dedicating ourselves to truly listening, we unlock the potential for deeper understanding, empathy, and mutual respect in all our relationships.

Expressing Needs Clearly and Compassionately

In any relationship, communication is critical. The ability to express ourselves clearly and compassionately is crucial to maintaining a healthy and fulfilling bond. When we fail to communicate our needs, misunderstandings can arise, leading to resentment and a breakdown of the connection. In this section, we will explore practical techniques and insights that can help us communicate our needs effectively, fostering an environment of understanding and empathy that can transform our relationships for the better.

Articulating Personal Needs Without Blame: Compassionate communication is expressing oneself without making the other person feel guilty or blamed. It involves focusing on our own experiences, emotions, and needs instead of criticizing the other person's actions. By doing so, we create a safe and open space for dialogue where both parties can communicate freely without fearing being judged.

There are several techniques that one can use to practice compassionate communication. For instance, it is essential to frame our sentences to emphasize our feelings and needs rather than what we perceive as the other person's shortcomings. This can significantly reduce defensiveness and promote a more receptive exchange.

Another technique is to avoid using accusatory language or making assumptions about the other person's thoughts or intentions. Instead, we can ask questions and seek clarification to understand their perspective better. Doing so can build empathy and establish a deeper connection with the other person.

Compassionate communication is a powerful tool for building healthy relationships, resolving conflicts, and fostering a sense of mutual respect and understanding. With practice and patience, we can all learn to communicate in a way that promotes harmony, growth, and compassion.

Timing and Setting Matter: The timing and location in which we express our needs can be just as important as how we do so. Selecting a moment when both individuals are at ease and not preoccupied with other concerns can significantly enhance the likelihood of one's needs being acknowledged and appreciated. Similarly, a comfortable and private environment can help establish a secure, welcoming space promoting sincerity and openness.

The Power of "I" Statements: Regarding effective communication, using "I" statements can be one of the most useful tools in our toolkit. This technique involves phrasing our messages from our own perspective, emphasizing our own feelings and needs. Doing so allows us to convey our personal emotions and requests non-confrontationally without blaming others. For instance, instead of saying, "You never tell me when you're going to be home, so I can't plan meals," we could say, "I feel anxious when I don't know your schedule because it makes it difficult for me to plan meals." This way, we are still expressing our concerns, but in a way that is more likely to foster understanding and empathy. I'd like to know more about this in the next section below.

Embracing Vulnerability: At the core of every healthy relationship lies the ability to express one's needs and desires. While opening up about our innermost feelings may seem daunting, it is a crucial step toward building a stronger emotional connection with our partners. Vulnerability is vital to fostering intimacy and understanding, and it invites our partners to delve deeper into our inner world, which can lead to a greater sense of empathy and compassion. By sharing our needs, we allow our loved ones to understand us more profoundly, which can lead to a more fulfilling and satisfying relationship. Expressing our emotions can create a safe space for honest communication and help bridge any gaps in understanding that may have existed previously. Vulnerability is a powerful tool that can help us build and maintain healthy, long-lasting relationships based on mutual trust and respect.

Integrating these principles into our daily interactions enhances our ability to communicate effectively and build a more empathetic and understanding relationship. Clear, compassionate expression of needs is not just about avoiding conflict; it's about nurturing a connection that thrives on mutual respect and understanding.

The "I" Statements Technique: Owning Your Feelings

The art of communication in relationships often hinges on how we express our feelings. The "I" statements technique is powerful in this endeavor, helping individuals take responsibility for their feelings and reducing defensiveness in their partners. This section explores the structure, purpose, and effective use of "I" statements in fostering healthier dialogues.

Structure and Purpose: When we communicate with our partners or anyone else, it's essential to use language that is clear, constructive, and non-confrontational. "I" statements are a communication technique that can help achieve these goals. "I" statements are phrases that begin with

"I feel," "I need," or "I want." These statements focus on the speaker's feelings and needs rather than their partner's actions or the person they're speaking with. By framing statements in this way, the emphasis is placed on personal experience and perception, which can help take ownership of one's emotions and reduce the likelihood of the listener feeling attacked or defensive.

Using "I" statements can also promote a more positive and constructive conversation. We create a safer space for open and honest communication when we express our feelings and needs clearly and non-confrontationally. This can lead to a deeper understanding of each other's perspectives and needs and ultimately strengthen the connection and trust in the relationship.

Transforming Statements: When conversing, we must be mindful of our language. Accusatory or generalized statements can often lead to conflict escalation. However, transforming these statements into "I" statements can change the dynamic of a conversation and foster a more productive dialogue. For instance, instead of saying, "You never listen to me," one might say, "I feel disregarded when I speak, and it seems like my words are not being heard." By using a personalized expression, the speaker can clearly convey the impact of the behavior and articulate a need without placing blame. This approach can help avoid misunderstandings, reduce tension, and promote mutual respect in any conversation.

Practical Exercises: To improve your communication skills and build stronger relationships, learning the art of using "I" statements is essential. The "I" statement technique involves expressing your thoughts and feelings in a non-threatening manner without placing blame on others. It is a powerful way of taking responsibility for your emotions and expressing them healthily and constructively.

To master the "I" statement technique, it's important to practice regularly. You can start by converting accusatory sentences into "I" statements, which allows you to take ownership of your feelings and express them clearly. Another effective way to improve your skill is role-playing scenarios where "I" statements would be beneficial. You can practice these exercises with a partner, friend, or even alone in front of a mirror.

Engaging in these activities can enhance your communication skills and build empathy and understanding between partners. It's a simple yet effective way to transform negative interactions into positive ones and to create deeper connections with the people around you.

Long-term Benefits: Using "I" statements is a powerful communication technique that can significantly improve the quality of relationships. When you consistently use "I" statements, you create a culture of openness and respect within the relationship. It encourages honest and vulnerable expression of feelings and needs, laying the groundwork for resolving conflicts healthily and constructively.

"I" statements are about taking ownership of your emotions and expressing them non-judgmentally. For example, instead of saying, "You always interrupt me when I'm talking," you could say, "I feel frustrated when I'm interrupted because I don't feel heard." This helps avoid blaming or attacking the other person and instead focuses on your feelings and needs.

Over time, using "I" statements can deepen the connection and mutual respect between partners. It makes both people feel heard and understood, leading to more effective problem-solving and a stronger emotional bond. By creating a safe space for honest and vulnerable expression, you build a foundation of trust and respect that can help to sustain a healthy and fulfilling relationship.

Embracing "I" statements is not just about altering how we speak; it's about changing our approach to conflict and connection. By owning and expressing our feelings constructively, we open the door to more meaningful and respectful communication.

Bridging the Gap: From Misunderstanding to Mutual Understanding

Mutual understanding is a crucial aspect of any healthy relationship, personal or professional. It is not something that happens automatically but rather a journey that requires proactive efforts from both parties. Achieving mutual understanding requires multiple factors, such as patience, clarity, and a genuine willingness to adopt the other person's perspective. It is an essential step that moves relationships from a place of misunderstanding and confusion to a haven of mutual comprehension and respect.

Building mutual understanding is a complex process that involves active listening, effective communication, and empathy. It requires taking the time to truly understand the other person's point of view, their needs, and their expectations. Active listening involves giving your undivided attention to the other person, asking clarifying questions, and summarizing what you have heard to ensure you understand correctly. Effective communication involves expressing yourself clearly and concisely, using language that is easy to understand, and avoiding misunderstandings. Empathy is the ability to put yourself in someone else's shoes and understand their feelings, motivations, and perspectives.

Several actionable strategies and concepts can be employed to bridge the gap between different perspectives and achieve mutual understanding. These include developing open-mindedness, avoiding assumptions and stereotypes, practicing active listening, and expressing oneself effectively. Recognizing and respecting the differences between individuals, cultures, and backgrounds is also essential. These strategies can help build trust, respect, and collaboration and create a foundation for healthy and successful relationships.

Strategies for Clarification: When addressing misunderstandings, it's essential to maintain a calm and constructive tone to prevent the escalation of tensions. One way to achieve this is by approaching each conversation with a mindset of understanding rather than focusing solely on being understood. Using neutral language and asking open-ended questions can help clarify any issues that may have arisen while avoiding language that may make the other person feel defensive. By doing so, both parties can work towards a resolution that is productive, respectful, and conducive to a positive outcome.

Perception Checking: Perception checking is a communication technique that involves verifying whether our understanding of a message from our partner is accurate. It is a valuable tool in ensuring we have correctly grasped our partner's point of view and intended message. To implement this technique, we summarize what our partner said to us and ask them to confirm whether our understanding is correct. This approach helps to prevent misunderstandings and misinterpretations that can often lead to conflict or frustration in relationships. Additionally, it demonstrates to our partner that we are actively engaged and interested in understanding their perspective, which can foster positive communication and strengthen the relationship.

Negotiating Shared Meanings: To achieve common ground, it's important to negotiate and agree on shared meanings while acknowledging and respecting each partner's viewpoints. This means taking the time to have a constructive conversation where each partner can express their thoughts and feelings. It's important to listen actively to what the other person is saying and to avoid interrupting or dismissing their ideas.

During the conversation, there may be points of disagreement. In these cases, it's essential to approach the situation calmly and respectfully. One way to do this is to find a compromise that both parties can agree on. Sometimes, it may be necessary to simply agree to disagree respectfully.

The ultimate goal of this process is to reach a mutual understanding that honors the relationship and each individual within it. This means finding a solution that works for both partners and meets their needs. By having a constructive conversation and working together towards a common goal, partners can build a solid and healthy relationship based on mutual respect and understanding.

The Importance of Regular Check-ins: Maintaining a healthy, happy relationship requires effort and communication. One effective way to prevent minor misunderstandings from escalating into more significant conflicts is by regularly checking in with each other. These check-ins provide a safe space for open dialogue, allowing both partners to express their concerns, share their feelings, and adjust their expectations. By actively listening to each other and addressing potential issues promptly, couples can proactively nurture their relationship and ensure that both partners feel heard and valued. This approach can also help build trust and strengthen the bond between partners, leading to a happier and more fulfilling relationship.

By integrating effective communication strategies into your interactions with others, you can transform misunderstandings into valuable opportunities for growth and deeper connection. These strategies include active listening, expressing empathy, and seeking clarification when needed. When you approach communication with the goal of mutual understanding, you create a safe and respectful space for dialogue. This foundation can lead to more meaningful, fulfilling relationships built on respect, trust, and love. Through open and honest communication, you can better understand one another's perspectives, needs, and desires. This understanding allows you to navigate challenges together, build stronger bonds, and create a shared vision for your future together.

Conflict De-escalation Strategies That Work

In any relationship, conflicts are inevitable. However, it's important to navigate through them to prevent them from escalating out of control. Effective de-escalation strategies are crucial for this purpose. These strategies help prevent the situation from worsening and set the stage for constructive resolution. By calming tense situations and fostering a positive outcome, relationships can be strengthened, and conflicts can be resolved healthily. This section provides practical techniques and insights for successfully de-escalating conflicts, which can be applied in various situations to resolve conflicts productively and positively.

Practical Techniques for Calming Tense Situations: In emotionally charged situations, taking a step back and creating some space between the parties involved can be helpful. One technique to achieve this is to take a timeout, allowing each individual to calm down and collect their thoughts before continuing the conversation. Alternatively, humor can diffuse tension, but it's essential to exercise caution and ensure that it does not come at the expense of the other person's feelings. Taking a break or using humor can effectively manage intense emotions and navigate difficult conversations with greater ease.

Self-Regulation and Emotional Awareness: It is crucial to manage your emotions and maintain a calm demeanor, especially in tense situations, to prevent conflicts from escalating. This requires identifying the factors that provoke emotional responses and utilizing techniques like taking deep breaths or engaging in positive self-talk to stay in control. By doing so, you can effectively diffuse the situation and avoid any adverse consequences that may arise from an uncontrolled emotional outburst.

Recognizing Signs of Escalation: It is crucial to be aware of the early warning signs of a conflict that is starting to escalate. These signs often manifest in sudden behavioral changes, such as heightened voices, rapid speech, or aggressive body language. I would like you to know these signs early on so you can take the appropriate action before the situation worsens. Effective de-escalation techniques like active listening, empathy, and assertive communication can help calm the problem and prevent it from escalating into a dangerous or violent confrontation. Prompt intervention can diffuse tensions and create a safe and respectful environment for all parties involved.

Empathy in De-escalation: Empathy can be a powerful tool for de-escalation in situations where conflicts arise. It involves understanding and appreciating the other person's point of view, even if you don't necessarily agree with it. Acknowledging their feelings and perspectives can help diffuse tension and create a more harmonious resolution. Several exercises, such as role reversal or active listening, can help enhance empathetic responses. Role reversal involves putting yourself in the other person's shoes and imagining how you would feel if you were in their situation. On the other hand, active listening requires you to give your full attention to the other person, asking questions to clarify their point of view and demonstrating that you value their input. These exercises can be invaluable tools during conflict, helping to foster understanding and create a more positive outcome for everyone involved.

To successfully implement conflict-resolution strategies, practicing and exercising patience is essential. The process can be challenging and requires a great deal of effort, but the positive impact on relationship health and communication is well worth it. By prioritizing de-escalation and seeking to understand the other person's perspective, conflicts can be transformed into opportunities for growth and deeper connection. Rather than causing division, conflicts can strengthen relationships and foster greater understanding. It's essential to remember that this process may take time, but the rewards are immense with persistence.

Conclusion

As we come to the end of this chapter on building an effective communication foundation, we have explored the intricacies of active listening, the importance of expressing our needs clearly and compassionately, the effectiveness of using "I" statements, and the essential strategies for de-escalation. Each section has provided practical insights and exercises to improve our communication skills to foster deeper understanding and connection in our relationships.

Looking ahead, Chapter 4 on Emotional Intelligence and Regulation will delve deeper into the internal factors that influence our external interactions. Understanding and managing our emotions is crucial for maintaining healthy, meaningful relationships. The upcoming chapter will explore how emotional intelligence can be developed to enrich our lives and the lives of those around us.

To encapsulate our journey through effective communication, let's reflect on the words of Stephen R. Covey from the start of the chapter: *"Most people do not listen with the intent to understand; they listen with the intent to reply."* As we move forward, we should strive to truly listen, understand, and connect on a level, transcending mere words.

Chapter Four

Emotional Intelligence and Regulation

"Between stimulus and response there is a space. In that space is our power to choose our response. In our response lies our growth and our freedom."

Viktor E. Frankl

Recognizing and Managing Trigger Points

In any relationship, it is essential to have a clear understanding of trigger points. Trigger points are specific situations or circumstances that can prompt a strong emotional response in an individual. These emotional responses can sometimes be disproportionate to the problem at hand, and they can significantly affect the dynamics of a relationship. Understanding trigger points requires an understanding of the psychological underpinnings that influence them. These can include past experiences, learned behaviors, and cognitive biases. By recognizing and addressing these underlying factors, individuals can better manage their trigger points and avoid unnecessary conflicts in their relationships. Managing trigger points effectively requires proactive strategies, such as emotional regulation techniques, communication skills, and boundary-setting. By utilizing these practical strategies, individuals can navigate the complex landscape of emotions in relationships and build stronger, healthier connections with others.

Understanding Trigger Points: Trigger points are specific emotional responses that we feel in certain situations and can be deeply personal. They are often rooted in past experiences or insecurities and can be challenging to identify. These triggers can be compared to emotional mines that, when stepped on, can explode into conflict. Recognizing these triggers in ourselves and our partners is the first step towards managing our emotional landscape more effectively. By becoming more aware of our triggers, we can work to prevent ourselves from getting overwhelmed by our emotions and respond more constructively. This can lead to more effective communication, better relationships, and a greater sense of emotional stability.

Mapping Triggers as a Preventive Measure: Couples often face emotional challenges that can strain their relationship. Identifying and understanding both personal and partner's trigger points can help them navigate the complex terrain of emotions. A trigger point can be any situation, behavior, or action that evokes a strong emotional response in an individual. By becoming aware of these triggers, couples can preemptively address potential issues before they escalate. Understanding each other's trigger points can promote effective communication and help couples build a stronger and more fulfilling relationship. It is important to remember that trigger points can vary from person to person, and what may be a trigger for one partner may not be for the other. Therefore, taking the time to learn and understand each other's trigger points is crucial to building a healthy and lasting relationship.

Techniques for Self-Soothing: In times of stress or emotional distress, it can be difficult to maintain a sense of calm and composure. However, being able to regulate one's own emotions is a valuable skill that can bring immense benefits to one's emotional and mental well-being. It involves recognizing when one's emotions are heightened and taking steps to soothe them before they spiral out of control.

Some techniques that can help in this process include deep breathing exercises, which can help slow down the body's physiological response to stress, and mindfulness practices that allow one to stay present and grounded in the moment. Positive self-talk, too, can be a helpful tool in fostering a sense of self-compassion and reducing feelings of anxiety or self-doubt.

Ultimately, taking responsibility for one's own emotional responses is a crucial part of this process. Rather than blaming external circumstances or other individuals for their own feelings, individuals who can regulate their emotions take ownership of their reactions and learn to respond more positively and constructively. This can lead to better relationships, improved communication, and a feeling of greater inner peace and contentment.

Communicating About and Negotiating Around Trigger Points: Effective communication is the cornerstone of any healthy and thriving relationship. A critical aspect of open communication is the discussion of trigger points with your partner. Trigger points refer to specific situations or actions that may lead to negative emotional responses or behavior in one or both partners. Being able to openly and honestly discuss these trigger points with your partner can foster a deeper understanding and mutual support, leading to a stronger and more resilient emotional foundation in the relationship. This kind of dialogue involves negotiating around these triggers in a way that respects both partners' needs and boundaries.

It is essential to acknowledge that trigger points are unique to each individual and can vary widely. For instance, one partner may have a history of trauma that makes certain topics or behaviors particularly triggering. In contrast, another partner may have a deep-seated fear of abandonment that seemingly innocuous situations can activate. By engaging in open and honest communication about trigger points, partners can become more attuned to each other's emotional needs and work together to navigate challenging situations. This can help build a more profound sense of connection and trust in the relationship and provide a solid foundation for long-term growth and fulfillment.

Managing trigger points can prevent overreactions and foster emotional regulation for healthier relationships.

The Role of Mindfulness in Emotional Regulation

When it comes to relationships, developing mindfulness skills can be immensely beneficial for managing emotions and improving our ability to stay present and patient, particularly in moments of conflict. Mindfulness practices can significantly impact our emotional landscape, transforming how we engage with our partners and enhancing the quality of our interactions. We can learn to respond to our partner's needs with greater understanding, compassion, and empathy by cultivating awareness and acceptance of our thoughts, feelings, and bodily sensations. We can create a more harmonious and fulfilling relationship with our loved ones with greater emotional regulation and self-awareness.

Introducing Mindfulness Practices: Mindfulness techniques effectively regulate our emotions and bring more balance to our relationships. By practicing focused breathing, meditation, and mindful listening, we can cultivate greater awareness and presence in our interactions. These techniques help us to stay grounded, centered, and attentive, even in challenging or stressful situations. We can foster deeper connections and build more meaningful relationships by staying in the moment and fully engaging with others. By incorporating mindfulness into our daily routine, we can develop greater emotional intelligence and become more effective communicators, leading to more positive and fulfilling relationships.

Benefits of Mindfulness: Practicing mindfulness can significantly impact how we react to our partner's words and actions. It allows us to create a momentary pause and thoughtfully choose our response instead of reacting habitually. This space for choice is crucial in cultivating more thoughtful and less reactive responses, which can significantly enhance the overall quality of our engagements with our partner. When we practice mindfulness, we become more aware of our thoughts and emotions, allowing us to respond more intentionally and compassionately rather than simply reacting impulsively. By being mindful of our responses, we can foster deeper connections and build more fulfilling relationships.

Mindfulness Exercises for Couples: Engaging in mindfulness practices as a couple can be a powerful way to enhance your emotional connection and empathy towards each other. There are several impactful exercises that you can try, such as synchronized breathing, shared meditation sessions, or simply engaging in mindful conversations. These activities can help you become more present and attuned to your partner's emotional state, leading to a deeper understanding of each other's thoughts and feelings. Practicing mindfulness together can reinforce the emotional bond and improve communication, ultimately leading to a more fulfilling and harmonious relationship.

Integrating Mindfulness into Daily Interactions: Mindfulness is a powerful tool that can be integrated into daily life to change one's relationships positively. When couples practice mindfulness, they gradually develop a greater awareness of their thoughts and emotions, which can help them better understand each other's perspective and navigate conflicts more constructively. This can lead to a transformation of conflict dynamics as couples shift from reactive patterns to responses characterized by understanding, empathy, and patience. By consistently practicing mindfulness, couples can cultivate a deeper level of connection, trust, and intimacy in their relationship, which can significantly impact their overall well-being and happiness. Over time, practicing mindfulness can help create a more harmonious and fulfilling partnership where both individuals feel seen, heard, and valued.

Couples can overcome emotional complexities and conflicts with greater ease by practicing mindfulness, laying the foundation for a resilient and emotionally intelligent relationship.

Techniques for Calming Down: From Tension to Tranquility

When conflicts arise in any relationship, feeling tense and on edge is natural. However, quickly transitioning from that state of tension to one of tranquility is desirable and essential for maintaining a healthy and meaningful relationship. A well-stocked toolkit of calming techniques can significantly alter the emotional climate and create an environment where constructive dialogue can flourish. These techniques can include deep breathing exercises, meditation, physical activity, or simply taking a moment to step away from the situation and calm down before returning to it with a fresh perspective. By employing these techniques, you can create a space where both you and the other person feel heard, understood, and appreciated and where disagreements can be resolved respectfully and productively.

Diverse Calming Techniques: In times of stress, having a toolkit of techniques to turn to for relief and relaxation can be helpful. Among the most effective strategies are deep breathing exercises, visualization, and physical grounding methods.

Deep breathing exercises can help regulate the autonomic nervous system, which controls our fight or flight response. By taking slow, deep breaths, we can activate the parasympathetic nervous system, which promotes relaxation and calmness. Visualization is another powerful tool for calming the mind and reducing stress. By visualizing a peaceful scene or environment, we can create a mental escape from the stressors of everyday life. This can help reduce anxiety and promote inner peace and tranquility. Physical grounding methods, such as yoga or tai chi, can also effectively reduce stress and promote relaxation. These practices help us reconnect with the present moment and our physical bodies, which can be grounding and centering.

Overall, each technique offers a unique pathway away from tension and towards greater calmness and relaxation. By incorporating them into our daily routines, we can build greater resilience and cope more effectively with stress and anxiety.

Recognizing Early Signs of Escalation: To achieve the desired outcome of calmness, detecting the early signs of emotional escalation is essential. These signs can be different for each individual. However, some common indicators include restlessness, increased heart rate, shallow breathing, muscle tension, sweating, and difficulty concentrating. Recognizing these signs and symptoms can help individuals proactively implement calming techniques, such as deep breathing, progressive muscle relaxation, visualization, mindfulness, and other stress-management strategies. By doing so, they can prevent the escalation of emotions and avoid reaching a point where they lose control of their thoughts and behaviors. This approach can be particularly helpful in situations that tend to trigger intense emotional responses, such as conflicts, stress, anxiety, or fear.

Creating a Personalized Calm-Down Plan: Developing a tailored calm-down plan that is personalized to fit individual triggers and responses is an effective way to manage emotionally charged moments. This approach ensures that the techniques used are accessible and effective when needed. Individuals can develop strategies that work best for them by identifying and understanding personal triggers. This may include deep breathing exercises, meditation, physical activity, or other coping mechanisms. The personalized approach to developing a calm-down plan can help reduce stress and anxiety and provide a sense of control during challenging situations. By having a plan, individuals are better equipped to navigate emotionally charged moments and achieve greater well-being.

The Power of Co-regulation: In a healthy partnership, both individuals can provide emotional support to each other through co-regulation. This process involves recognizing and responding to each other's emotional states to promote a sense of safety and security within the relationship. When one partner is distressed, the other can help guide them back to a calm state by providing a listening ear, offering comfort, and providing reassurance. This strengthens the emotional connection between partners and enhances their understanding of each other's needs and emotions. Ultimately, co-regulation can help partners maintain balance and stability in their relationship, even during difficult times.

By embracing effective conflict resolution techniques, individuals and couples can transform their interactions, leading to more peaceful and productive relationships.

Empathy: Walking in Your Partner's Shoes

Empathy is an essential aspect of any healthy and successful relationship. It involves the ability to understand and share our partners' feelings, perspectives, and needs. When we cultivate empathy, we become better equipped to navigate conflicts, communicate effectively, and build a deeper connection with our loved ones. The psychological underpinnings of empathy are complex and multifaceted. Research shows that empathy combines emotional and cognitive processes, involving both affective and cognitive empathy. Affective empathy refers to the ability to share and experience the emotional states of others. In contrast, cognitive empathy involves understanding and identifying with another's perspective without necessarily feeling the emotions that they are experiencing.

Empathy plays a critical role in fostering intimacy, trust, and mutual understanding in relationships. It allows us to communicate more effectively and resolve conflicts more constructively and respectfully. However, empathy is not always easy to cultivate. It requires patience, practice, and an open mind. Fortunately, there are practical ways to nurture empathy in relationships. One of the most effective ways is to actively listen to our partners and try to see things from their perspective. We can also practice expressing empathy through nonverbal cues, such as eye contact, nodding, and facial expressions. Additionally, engaging in activities that promote emotional awareness, such as meditation and mindfulness, can help us develop greater empathy and emotional intelligence.

Understanding Empathy: Empathy is a complex concept encompassing emotional and cognitive dimensions. It's not limited to just feeling with someone but also to understanding their thoughts and emotions from their point of view. Empathy plays a vital role in healthy relationships by enabling us to respond to our partners with care and understanding. When we empathize with our partner, we can put ourselves in their shoes and see things from their perspective. This ability helps us to connect with them on a deeper level and build stronger relationships. Empathy involves being present in the moment, listening attentively, and responding with kindness and compassion. It's a crucial component of healthy relationships that helps us to navigate difficult situations with our partners and fosters a more profound sense of connection and understanding.

Enhancing Empathetic Listening and Understanding: Exercises like role reversal and deep listening sessions can prove extremely helpful when it comes to developing empathy. In role reversal exercises, partners switch roles in a conversation, taking turns as the listener and the speaker. This can help each partner understand the other's perspective and appreciate their point of view. On the other hand, deep listening sessions involve focusing entirely on understanding the partner's feelings without immediately responding. This kind of listening requires high concentration and attentiveness and can help partners better understand each other's experiences. Couples can improve their communication skills by practicing these exercises regularly and building a stronger, more empathetic relationship.

Empathy in Apology and Reconciliation: The foundation of effective apologies and reconciliation processes is empathy. To offer a genuine apology and facilitate healing, it is essential to comprehend and accept the consequences of one's actions on one's partner. It requires more than just uttering the words "I'm sorry." Instead, it necessitates demonstrating a comprehensive understanding of how the action has affected the partner. This process involves actively listening to the partner's experience, acknowledging their pain, and showing empathy by putting oneself in their shoes. Only then can one take responsibility for their actions and work towards repairing the relationship.

Maintaining Empathy Amidst Disagreement: Regarding disagreements or defensive moments in a conversation, keeping empathy at the forefront can be challenging. Nevertheless, it is essential to do so, as it can help resolve the issue and maintain a healthy relationship. One of the most effective strategies to maintain empathy is to take a moment to reflect on the partner's perspective. This can help you understand their viewpoint and the reasoning behind their opinions or actions. It is also crucial to avoid making assumptions, which can be misleading and lead to misunderstandings. Instead, one must ask clarifying questions to understand their viewpoint fully. This way, you can have a more constructive conversation and find common ground to move forward.

Couples can enhance their relationship by making a conscious effort to develop empathy. This involves attempting to understand and empathize with one another, leading to a stronger bond built on mutual respect and understanding. It requires walking in each other's shoes, seeing the world from their perspective, and working together towards a common goal.

Transforming Negative Emotions into Constructive Conversations

In our society, negative emotions are often seen as obstacles that hinder our growth and progress. However, recent research has shown that these emotions can catalyze personal and relational growth. When we properly recognize and manage negative emotions, they offer us unique opportunities for constructive dialogue and mutual understanding. Negative emotions can help us deepen our connections with others. When we are vulnerable and share our negative emotions with someone we trust, it can create a space for them to do the same. This can lead to more authentic and intimate relationships.

Turning negative emotions into relational strengths requires first acknowledging and accepting our own emotions. It is essential to understand that negative emotions are a natural part of the human experience and that everyone experiences them occasionally. We can then use active listening, empathy, and validation techniques to communicate our emotions effectively to others. Using these techniques, we can turn what was once a source of conflict and tension into an opportunity for growth and deeper connection within our relationships. So, the next time you face negative emotions, don't shy away from them - embrace them and use them as a personal and relational development tool.

Identifying Underlying Needs and Fears: Delving into their underlying causes is crucial to handling negative emotions effectively. Many times, these emotions stem from unfulfilled needs or deep-seated fears. Identifying these triggers is the first step towards a more compassionate and personalized way of dealing with emotional concerns. Pinpointing the root causes makes it easier to approach the situation with empathy and a more targeted approach.

Techniques for Collaborative Expression: Effectively communicating negative emotions is crucial in maintaining healthy relationships, whether they are personal or professional. The key to constructively expressing negative emotions is avoiding assigning blame and focusing on using "I" statements that convey your feelings. This approach encourages collaboration and understanding rather than conflict and defensiveness. By suggesting constructive pathways forward, you can effectively address the underlying issues and work towards a resolution that benefits everyone involved. It is important to remember that expressing negative emotions does not have to be a negative experience, and by using effective communication techniques, you can foster positive interactions that promote growth and understanding.

Creating a Safe Emotional Space: Creating a safe and nurturing environment is critical for any successful relationship. This is especially true when it comes to navigating through the tough times. To build a strong foundation, it's essential for both partners to feel comfortable sharing their feelings without fear of judgment. This safe space should encourage openness, understanding, and validation, making it easier to navigate through negative emotions together. When both partners feel safe and supported, it can help build trust, increase intimacy, and ultimately lead to a stronger and more fulfilling relationship.

Emotional Alchemy: Emotional alchemy is a concept that emphasizes the possibility of transforming negative emotions into positive relational outcomes. This transformation is made possible by conscious communication and mutual support between partners. When couples work together to understand and address the root cause of negative emotions, they can deepen their connection and strengthen their relationship. By fostering resilience and building a strong foundation of trust and understanding, partners can navigate life's challenges together and grow as individuals and a couple. Emotional alchemy requires patience, compassion, and a willingness to engage in open and honest dialogue, but the rewards are often profound and long-lasting.

Couples can benefit from positively approaching negative emotions. Instead of treating them as obstacles, they can view them as opportunities to communicate, understand each other better, and strengthen their relationship. Couples can build a deeper and more meaningful connection by adopting this approach.

Conclusion

This chapter has explored the complex process of emotional intelligence and regulation. It has emphasized the importance of identifying and managing trigger points, the transformative effects of mindfulness, techniques for de-escalating tension, the powerful nature of empathy, and the skill of transforming negative emotions into constructive dialogues. Each section offered practical strategies for enhancing understanding and fostering connection in relationships.

I'm looking forward to Chapter 5: Conflict Resolution Frameworks; we'll go into structured approaches to resolving conflicts, providing readers with more tools for building harmonious relationships.

To summarize this chapter's essence, let's reflect on Viktor E. Frankl's words: 'Between stimulus and response, there is a space. In that space lies our power to choose our response. Our response determines our growth and freedom.' This quote beautifully captures the chapter's central theme of utilizing emotional intelligence and regulation to navigate complex relationships with grace and intention.

Chapter Five

Conflict Resolution Frameworks

Identifying the Root Causes of Conflicts

In any relationship, conflicts are inevitable. However, many conflicts are not just mere disagreements between two people; they are symptoms of deeper, underlying issues that need to be addressed for a lasting resolution. For instance, a simple argument about household chores may result from one partner feeling undervalued or unsupported in the relationship. Recognizing and understanding these root causes is crucial in navigating conflicts toward productive outcomes.

Peeling back the layers of conflict to reveal underlying needs and fears is a vital step in resolving the issues. When we allow ourselves to be vulnerable and express our emotions honestly, we create an opportunity to connect with our partner on a deeper level. This, in turn, can help us understand each other's perspectives and needs better. Fostering open and honest dialogue is essential in resolving conflicts. Creating a safe and non-judgmental space where both partners can express their thoughts and feelings without fear of being criticized or judged is crucial. Active listening, empathy, and validation are essential to productive communication during conflict resolution.

Patience and non-judgment are also significant in exploring underlying issues in a relationship. Sometimes, it may take several conversations or even therapy sessions to get to the root of the problem. It's essential to be patient and not rush the process, as building trust and intimacy in any relationship takes time. Finally, it's crucial to distinguish between surface-level irritants and core issues that fuel conflicts repeatedly. While surface-level conflicts may be resolved through simple communication and negotiation, deeper issues may require more significant changes and compromise in the relationship. By identifying the root cause of the conflict, couples can work towards creating a long-lasting and fulfilling relationship.

The Importance of Uncovering Underlying Needs and Fears

According to Gottman and Silver (2015[1]), conflicts in a relationship are often caused by unfulfilled needs or unresolved fears. To effectively address these underlying issues, it is essential to establish an environment of safety where both partners feel comfortable expressing their deepest concerns without fear of judgment or retaliation. This safe space enables an exploration of the root cause of the discord, which could be a need for emotional security, a fear of inadequacy, or any other underlying factor. By exploring and acknowledging these deeper concerns, couples can work together to resolve the issues and build a stronger, healthier relationship.

Strategies for Deep and Honest Exploration

When it comes to resolving conflicts, asking open-ended questions can be an incredibly effective approach. Rather than simply trying to identify and address surface-level issues, open-ended questions can help uncover the underlying causes of disagreements. By asking questions like "What needs of yours do you feel are not being met?" or "Can you explain why this issue is so important to you?" partners are encouraged to take a step back and reflect more deeply on their own perspectives and concerns. This can lead to a more productive and empathetic conversation where each partner feels heard and understood. Research has shown that using open-ended questions in conflict resolution can help partners build stronger relationships and improve their overall communication skills (Johnson, 2008[2]).

The Role of Patience and Non-Judgment

In discussions that involve deep-seated issues, it is essential to approach them with patience and a non-judgmental attitude. These conversations can be emotionally taxing, and it may take time to uncover the root of the problem. It is crucial to understand that the process of uncovering these issues may require a considerable amount of emotional labor and time. As an active listener, it is important to focus on understanding the speaker's perspective rather than immediately trying to fix or respond to their concerns. By listening and understanding, you can create a safe and supportive environment for the speaker to feel heard and validated.

Distinguishing Between Surface Issues and Core Problems

When resolving conflicts, it's essential to understand the immediate triggers and underlying issues clearly. Conflicts often arise due to surface irritants that may be frustrating to deal with, but these irritants are usually a manifestation of deeper, unresolved issues. By taking the time to identify and address the core problems that are fueling the conflict, you can develop more sustainable solutions. Identifying and resolving the underlying issues is often the key to building a stronger relationship with the other party involved. So, the next time you are faced with a conflict, take a step back and try to understand the root cause of the problem. By addressing the underlying issues, you can prevent similar conflicts from arising in the future.

When conflicts arise within relationships, it can be challenging to identify the root causes that are driving the issue. It requires a deep and empathetic exploration of the partners' underlying needs, fears, and desires. By asking open-ended questions, showing patience, and adopting a non-judgmental approach, couples can gradually distinguish between the superficial and the substantial aspects of their problems. This understanding is critical for achieving resolution and fostering a healthier, more fulfilling relationship. It enables partners to address the core issues causing the conflict and work together towards finding practical solutions. By being transparent and vulnerable with one another, couples can establish trust and intimacy, which are essential foundations for a strong and lasting relationship.

The Win-Win Scenario: Crafting Mutually Satisfying Solutions

When it comes to resolving conflicts in a relationship, it's important to seek true resolution. This involves finding solutions that are mutually beneficial and take into account the needs and desires of both partners. It's not enough to simply "win" the argument or to have one person's needs met at the expense of the other. Instead, true resolution requires a willingness to compromise and to work together towards a solution that respects the needs of both individuals. By crafting fair and equitable outcomes, both partners can feel heard and valued, and the relationship can be strengthened as a result. Ultimately, the key to achieving true resolution is approaching conflict with an open mind and a willingness to collaborate to find the best possible outcome for everyone involved.

Interest-Based Negotiation

The concept of interest-based negotiation emphasizes the significance of concentrating on mutual interests rather than entrenched positions. This approach, introduced by Fisher, Ury, and Patton (2011[3]), encourages partners to look beyond the immediate issue and identify what they truly need from the resolution. By doing so, both parties can work together to find a solution that meets the needs of all involved rather than focusing on their own individual wants or desires. This approach is instrumental in complex negotiations, where multiple issues may be at play, and it can help build stronger, more collaborative relationships between negotiating partners. Overall, the interest-based negotiation approach is an effective way to achieve win-win outcomes that benefit everyone involved.

Brainstorming Solutions Together

When resolving conflicts or finding solutions to problems in a relationship, it is crucial to approach the matter with a collaborative mindset. Brainstorming together is an effective way to address the issues at hand and come up with solutions that can cater to the needs and interests of both partners. This process involves a lot of open communication, active listening, and creative thinking to explore all possible outcomes that could satisfy both parties. It requires mutual respect, understanding, and a willingness to compromise. By working together and considering each other's perspectives, couples can find solutions that not only resolve the problem at hand but also strengthen their relationship and build a deeper level of trust and intimacy.

Examples of Win-Win Solutions

When it comes to resolving common relationship conflicts, adopting a win-win approach that seeks to benefit both partners can be helpful. One effective way to demonstrate the practical application of this approach is to provide examples of win-win solutions that have worked in similar situations. For instance, if one partner wants more quality time together while the other desires personal space, a win-win solution could involve setting aside specific times for shared activities while respecting each other's need for individual time. This might mean scheduling date nights on certain days of the week or month while allowing each partner some alone time to pursue their interests or hobbies. By finding a mutually agreeable solution that honors both partners' needs, couples can strengthen their bond and foster a more harmonious relationship.

Flexibility and Creativity in Solution Finding

In any collaborative effort, it is imperative to maintain flexibility and creativity in the search for mutually satisfying solutions. This entails being open to compromise and considering unconventional options that may effectively fulfill the needs of both partners. Maintaining a positive attitude toward exploring new solutions can lead to a more productive and successful negotiation. By being flexible in your approach, you can allow for unexpected and innovative solutions that may have yet to be initially considered. This approach fosters collaboration and allows both parties to feel heard and valued in the decision-making process. It also helps to build stronger relationships based on trust and mutual respect. Ultimately, maintaining an open mind and a willingness to explore alternative solutions can lead to more successful and satisfying outcomes for both parties.

When it comes to resolving conflicts in relationships, it's important to create scenarios that benefit both parties involved. This shift from focusing on individual interests to finding common ground can be achieved through collaborative problem-solving. This approach involves identifying mutual interests, brainstorming ideas together, and maintaining flexibility throughout the process. By doing so, couples can find innovative solutions that not only resolve their conflicts but also enhance their relationship as a whole. It's essential to remember that this approach requires open communication, active listening, and a willingness to compromise. With these qualities, couples can work together towards a positive outcome that benefits everyone involved.

Navigating Through High-Stakes Relationship Challenges

In every relationship, there exist certain conflicts that are of great significance due to their potential for profound impact. These challenges can significantly alter the course of a relationship, for better or worse, if not approached with care and consideration. Such conflicts may arise due to differences in values, needs, or expectations and can pose significant emotional and psychological challenges for both parties. Navigating these high-stakes conflicts with empathy, communication, and a willingness to compromise is crucial to maintaining a healthy and fulfilling relationship.

Identifying High-Stakes Challenges

In relationships, certain challenges can push the limits of the couple's commitment and resilience. These challenges can be high-stakes and may include issues such as infidelity, financial crises, or significant differences in life goals. When faced with these challenges, it becomes crucial for both partners to work together to find a solution that is in the best interest of their shared future. Infidelity can cause deep emotional wounds and erode the trust that is the foundation of a relationship. Financial crises can put a strain on the couple's financial stability and cause stress and anxiety. Differences in life goals can lead to conflicts and disagreements that may require compromise and mutual understanding. Ultimately, these challenges can be overcome with open communication, honesty, and a willingness to work together towards a shared future.

The Role of External Support

When dealing with complex and high-stakes issues in a relationship, seeking external support is crucial to help navigate them effectively. One option to consider is counseling or mediation, which provides a safe and structured environment for addressing these challenges. This approach offers valuable perspectives and strategies that go beyond what the couple may have at their immediate disposal. By working with a trained professional, couples can gain insights into their relationship patterns, learn effective communication techniques, and develop strategies for overcoming obstacles. Gottman & Silver (2015[4]) suggest that counseling or mediation can be a powerful tool for couples seeking to improve their relationship and overcome difficult challenges.

Strategies for Emotional Composure

Maintaining emotional composure and clarity is essential when faced with critical challenges. In such situations, it can be easy to get carried away by emotions, which may cloud our judgment and make it challenging to develop constructive solutions. To prevent this from happening, several techniques can help individuals stay grounded and focused. For instance, mindfulness can help one cultivate awareness and detachment from strong emotions, allowing them to respond more thoughtfully to challenging situations. On the other hand, deliberate communication involves taking the time to listen actively, understand others' perspectives, and express oneself clearly and respectfully. Lastly, emotional regulation techniques, such as deep breathing, visualization, or cognitive restructuring, can help individuals manage their emotional responses and avoid reactive behaviors that may aggravate the situation. By applying these techniques, individuals can better navigate critical challenges and work towards positive outcomes.

The Foundation of Shared Commitment

When it comes to maintaining a healthy and strong relationship, one of the most critical elements is the shared commitment to its future. This commitment is a solid foundation for tackling even the most challenging issues that may arise in the relationship. It is a promise that both individuals make to each other to work through any hurdle that comes their way rather than giving up and going their separate ways. This commitment is not just about weathering the storm together but also about the willingness to navigate difficulties and conflicts together. It highlights the importance of finding solutions that resolve the issue at hand and reinforce the bond between both individuals. When both parties are committed to the relationship's future, they are more likely to approach problems as a team rather than as individuals, strengthening the relationship's foundation.

Having a shared commitment to the relationship's future means that both individuals are willing to put in the effort and make the necessary sacrifices to ensure the relationship thrives. It is not just about the present but also about the long-term, and it requires both individuals to be patient, understanding, and supportive of each other. Ultimately, this commitment sets the foundation for a healthy, fulfilling, and long-lasting relationship.

Successfully navigating difficult challenges in relationships requires internal resilience and external support. Couples can work through these challenges together by identifying the nature of the issues they face, seeking appropriate external help, maintaining their emotional composure, and grounding their actions in a shared commitment. By taking these steps, they can find a path forward that works for both of them.

The Time-Out Technique: Knowing When to Pause

In moments of intense disputes or disagreements, it's crucial to take a strategic pause. Doing so can prevent any harmful actions or words that may be said in the heat of the moment. Pausing also creates space for reflection and allows for a calmer re-engagement with the situation. This approach can help ensure that decisions are well-considered and fair to all parties involved. Taking a strategic pause is a valuable tool for maintaining healthy relationships and constructively resolving conflicts.

Recognizing the Need for a Time-Out

When you're conversing with someone and notice that their anger is escalating, it might be a sign that it's time to take a break. Other physical symptoms of stress, such as a raised voice or a rapid heartbeat, can also indicate that a time-out might be beneficial. Sometimes, conversations can go in circles, and it can be difficult to make progress toward a resolution. In situations like these, recognizing the signs early can prevent further damage and create an opportunity for a more productive dialogue later. Taking a time-out can allow both parties to calm down and gather their thoughts, ultimately leading to a more successful and respectful conversation.

Initiating and Respecting a Time-Out

To effectively initiate a time-out during a conversation or a conflict, it is vital to have clear communication and mutual respect. One way to ensure this is by establishing a time-out agreement in advance, which can help set expectations and boundaries. This agreement should include details such as how to signal a time-out and each person's actions during this period. For instance, agreeing on a specific hand gesture or phrase that indicates the need for a time-out may be helpful. Additionally, each person may decide on their own self-care activities to engage in during the time-out period, such as taking a walk, meditating, or simply breathing deeply. By establishing a time-out agreement in advance, both parties can feel more in control of the situation and more confident in their ability to communicate effectively.

Using the Time-Out for Self-Reflection

Taking some time out during a conflict is a highly effective strategy for self-reflection and emotional regulation. It allows individuals to step back from the situation and gather their thoughts, feelings, and emotions. This period can be used to identify the root cause of the conflict and gain a fresh perspective on the matter at hand. Some practical techniques to calm down during this period include deep breathing exercises, journaling, or going for a walk. Deep breathing exercises can help to slow down the heart rate, lower blood pressure, and reduce stress levels. Journaling can be a helpful way to process emotions, organize thoughts, and gain clarity. Going for a walk is a great way to get some fresh air, clear the mind, and release tension. By taking the time to reflect and regulate emotions, individuals can approach conflicts more productively and positively.

Constructive Re-engagement After a Time-Out

When attempting to re-engage after a time-out, it's essential to approach the conversation calmly. This means keeping your emotions in check and avoiding aggressive or confrontational behavior. Instead, try to express a willingness to listen to the other person's point of view. This can be achieved by actively listening to what they have to say and acknowledging their feelings. It's also important to focus on resolving the conflict constructively. This means working towards a mutually beneficial solution that addresses the underlying issue. One way to do this is by openly communicating your thoughts and feelings while also being receptive to the other person's perspective. Also, avoiding bringing up past grievances during this conversation is essential. Doing so can derail the progress made toward resolving the current conflict and may cause the other person to become defensive or hostile. Instead, try to stay focused on the issue and work together towards finding a resolution that works for everyone involved.

The time-out technique helps couples better handle conflicts, resulting in stronger and more resilient relationships.

Repair and Recovery: Post-Conflict Strategies for Reconnection

After a conflict, people involved often feel hurt, upset, and disconnected from each other. However, the aftermath of the conflict can offer a unique opportunity for emotional repair and reconnection that can ultimately strengthen the relationship. This process of repair and reconnection can involve acknowledging and validating each other's feelings, expressing remorse and forgiveness, and working together to find solutions to prevent similar conflicts in the future. It requires patience, empathy, and open communication, but the result can be a deeper sense of trust, understanding, and closeness between the parties involved.

Acknowledging the Impact of Conflict

In any conflict, both partners must take the time to explicitly acknowledge and discuss the impact the situation has had on each of them. By doing so, they create a safe space to share their thoughts and feelings, ultimately leading to a greater understanding and empathy between them. This type of open communication is crucial for the healing process and can help to establish deeper levels of trust and respect within the relationship. By acknowledging and discussing the effects of the conflict on each person, partners are better equipped to move forward positively and productively.

Apologizing and Offering Forgiveness

Mistakes and misunderstandings will inevitably occur in any relationship, causing the need for apologies and forgiveness. The process of apologizing and offering forgiveness can play a crucial role in restoring trust, fostering healing, and reconnecting with one another.

When apologizing, it is vital to be sincere in your words and actions. A genuine apology should acknowledge the wrong that was done and express remorse for any hurt or harm caused. It is also important to be specific in your apologies, addressing the particular actions or words that caused the hurt or harm. On the other hand, forgiveness should be offered freely, without any conditions or expectations. Forgiveness can be a powerful tool in facilitating emotional closure for both partners, allowing them to move forward from the hurt and pain caused by the mistake or misunderstanding.

In summary, apologizing and offering forgiveness can be challenging, but it is critical to the success of any relationship. By being sincere, specific, and forgiving, partners can work together to heal and strengthen their bond for the future.

Rituals of Reconnection

Reestablishing intimacy and trust can be a complex and challenging process following a conflict in a relationship. However, couples can use certain rituals of reconnection to help restore their bond. These rituals can take many forms, such as engaging in shared activities or performing meaningful gestures with special significance for the couple. The purpose of these rituals is to provide tangible affirmations of the relationship's resilience and the partners' commitment to each other. By engaging in these rituals, the couple can demonstrate their willingness to put in the effort required to overcome challenges and maintain a strong and healthy relationship.

Post-Conflict Growth

Post-conflict growth is a concept that highlights the possibility for couples to utilize their conflicts and the resolution process as an opportunity to develop a more robust and resilient relationship. When partners learn from their conflicts, it can lead to a better understanding of each other's perspectives, allowing them to connect on a deeper emotional level. This, in turn, can strengthen the foundation of their relationship. Couples can foster a healthy relationship that can withstand future challenges by using conflicts to learn and grow together.

By implementing effective strategies for repairing and recovering from conflicts, one can take advantage of challenging situations and use them as opportunities for personal growth and relationship strengthening. This helps deepen the connection between individuals and reinforces the relationship's resilience and longevity.

Conclusion

In Chapter 5, we've explored a variety of frameworks and strategies for resolving conflicts within relationships, emphasizing the importance of understanding underlying issues, crafting win-win solutions, navigating high-stakes challenges, taking strategic pauses, and engaging in repair and recovery practices post-conflict. These approaches highlight the significance of empathy, communication, patience, and commitment to mutual growth and understanding.

Looking forward to Chapter 6, "Rebuilding Trust and Intimacy," we will delve into how couples can mend the fabric of their relationship after conflicts and breaches of trust. This next chapter will offer insights and actionable steps for healing emotional wounds, re-establishing trust, deepening intimacy, and fortifying the relationship's resilience against future challenges.

Make a Difference with Your Review

Unlock the Power of Generosity

> "In every shared moment of silence, a story of togetherness is woven."
>
> Evelyn A. Stonebridge

In the dance of life, the steps we take together matter the most. This book, "Relationship Conflict Resolution," is more than just pages bound together—it's a catalyst for change in your relationships. By learning to transform conflict into closeness, you hold the power to turn every argument into an opportunity for growth and intimacy.

Now, I extend a heartfelt invitation to you, a fellow traveler on the path of connection and understanding. Your voice can be a beacon for others navigating the complexities of their relationships.

Would you share the light of your experience by leaving a review?

Your insights can illuminate the path for someone else, a kindred spirit in search of guidance. Someone who, just like you, seeks harmony and deeper understanding with their partner.

Our mission is clear: to help each soul find peace and connection within their relationships. By sharing your thoughts, you become an integral part of this journey, helping to extend the reach of understanding and compassion.

Picture this: your review could be the key that unlocks someone else's heart, allowing love and trust to flourish where conflict once took root.

It's simple to spread this kindness. Just a few seconds of your time to leave a review can echo in countless lives. Here's how:

1. Scan the QR code below or visit https://geni.us/XdA6Yh.

2. Share your thoughts and experiences with the book.

https://geni.us/Xd A6Yh

Join our mission. Be the change you wish to see in relationships around you. And as we forge ahead, know that your support propels us forward into a future where every conflict is an open door to connection.

Thank you for being the spark that ignites change.

With gratitude, Evelyn A. Stonebridge

P.S. - Remember, each bit of wisdom you share multiplies and returns to you. If this book has touched your life, pass it on and watch the magic of generosity work its wonders.

Chapter Six

Rebuilding Trust and Intimacy

The Road to Rebuilding Trust: Transparency and Consistency

When a relationship has been marred by conflict or betrayal, rebuilding trust becomes an intricate and arduous process. Trust is the foundation of any meaningful bond, and when it's been damaged, it's necessary to embark on a journey towards reliability and assurance. This journey requires consistent actions and transparent communication, which can be challenging, but it also presents a chance for couples to deepen their connection and strengthen the resilience of their relationship. Through this process, both partners can learn to be more vulnerable, honest, and understanding towards each other, leading to a more profound and fulfilling partnership. It's a journey that requires patience, effort, and commitment, but the rewards of a stronger, more trustworthy bond are well worth it.

- **Admitting Faults and Making Amends:** Rebuilding trust is a challenging task that demands a proactive and sincere approach. The first step towards restoring trust is to honestly and openly acknowledge one's mistakes. This involves taking complete responsibility for the actions that led to the breakdown of trust, and demonstrating a genuine commitment to making things right. A sincere admission of wrongdoing is a crucial element of trust restoration. It sets the foundation for rebuilding the relationship by demonstrating accountability for one's actions and showing a willingness to make amends. By acknowledging one's mistakes in a transparent and sincere manner, it becomes easier to rebuild trust and restore the relationship to a better state.

- **Setting Clear Expectations for the Future:** Building trust between individuals in a relationship requires a foundation of shared objectives and goals for the future. Establishing unambiguous, universally accepted expectations is crucial in avoiding potential misunderstandings and ensuring that both parties are working together towards the same objectives.

- **The Importance of Patience and Time:** Rebuilding trust is a complex and delicate process that cannot be rushed. It involves a series of daily actions and decisions that consistently demonstrate one's unwavering commitment to the relationship and its underlying values. This requires a great deal of effort, time, and patience, as the process may be slow and gradual, and any misstep can potentially set back progress. In order to rebuild trust, one must be willing to listen, be empathetic, and show genuine concern for the other person's feelings. Additionally, it is important to be transparent, honest, and accountable, and to follow through on promises and commitments. Over time, these actions and decisions can help restore trust and strengthen the bond between individuals.

- **Demonstrating Transparency and Building Trust:** Establishing trust in any relationship is crucial, and transparency is an essential factor in its success. It requires being open about one's emotions, thoughts, and actions, ensuring that one's partner feels included and valued. To build trust and foster transparency, one may engage in behaviors such as frequent check-ins, collaboration in decision-making, and proactive communication about potential stressors or challenges that may arise. By doing so, partners can create a safe and secure environment, leading to a more fulfilling and satisfying relationship.

- **Embracing Vulnerability:** When we talk about building trust in a relationship, vulnerability is a powerful tool that can work wonders. It involves opening up to your partner and sharing your fears, insecurities, and hopes without any inhibitions. When partners are vulnerable with each other, it can foster a deeper emotional connection and mutual empathy, which in turn, can pave the way for a more intimate and robust relationship. Being vulnerable means allowing yourself to be seen and heard, even in moments of uncertainty or weakness. It requires courage and trust, but if done right, it can create a strong bond between partners that is built on honesty, understanding, and compassion.

Rebuilding trust and intimacy after a breach can be an uphill battle for couples, but it is also a testament to their resilience and unwavering commitment to each other. It requires a deep understanding of each other's needs, fears, and expectations, and a genuine willingness to put in the effort to heal and grow together.

Transparency and honesty are crucial in this journey. Both partners need to be open and forthcoming about their thoughts, feelings, and actions. Consistency is also key; small steps taken every day to rebuild trust and intimacy can go a long way in restoring the relationship. Vulnerability is another crucial component, as it allows couples to connect on a deeper level and truly understand each other's perspectives.

By focusing on these principles and integrating them into the relationship, couples can embark on a meaningful journey towards healing and growth, setting the stage for a deeper and more fulfilling connection. It may not be an easy journey, but it is one that can bring couples closer together and strengthen their bond in ways they never thought possible.

Apologies and Forgiveness: Healing Together

In the realm of human relationships, conflicts and misunderstandings are an inevitable part of life. However, what distinguishes healthy and successful relationships from strained ones is the ability to effectively apologize and forgive. Genuine apologies, the process of forgiveness, and self-forgiveness are all crucial components of healing and moving forward from past conflicts.

An effective apology is not just a mere expression of regret or a simple "I'm sorry." It requires a deep sense of sincerity, genuine remorse, and a strong commitment to making things right. It is a way to take responsibility for one's actions, acknowledging the harm caused, and making efforts to repair the damage done. Genuine apologies are vital for rebuilding trust and repairing damaged relationships. Forgiveness is a nuanced and complex process that involves acknowledging the pain and hurt caused by the offender, and choosing to move forward without seeking vengeance or punishment. It entails letting go of anger, bitterness, and resentment, and choosing to focus on positive emotions and experiences. Forgiveness is not a one-time event, but rather a journey that can take time and effort. It is a transformative process that requires both courage and compassion.

Self-forgiveness is a vital aspect of the healing process that often goes overlooked. It involves recognizing our own mistakes and shortcomings, accepting responsibility for our actions, and committing to personal growth and change. Self-forgiveness is a deeply personal and often challenging process that can be a crucial step towards healing and inner peace. Finally, releasing bitterness is an essential part of the process of healing and moving on from past conflicts. It involves letting go of negative emotions and experiences, and focusing on positive aspects of life. It is a pathway towards resilience, positivity, and a brighter future.

The Elements of a Sincere Apology

A genuine apology involves more than just saying "I'm sorry." It requires the acknowledgement of the hurt caused, taking full responsibility for one's actions, and a sincere commitment to change the behavior that caused the harm. By acknowledging and taking responsibility for the impact of one's actions, the person demonstrates empathy and a willingness to understand the other person's perspective. Finally, a commitment to change behavior shows that the person is not just sorry for the past, but also committed to prevent similar harm from happening in the future. Overall, a sincere apology is a process that involves humility, empathy, and a genuine desire to mend the relationship.

Understanding Forgiveness

Forgiveness is a multifaceted and intricate process that requires an individual to release any lingering grudges or animosity towards another person for a perceived wrongdoing. It is not a matter of disregarding or approving the harmful behavior, but rather of relinquishing oneself from the weight of past hurts to move forward in a positive direction. In essence, forgiveness is a liberating act that allows one to break free from the shackles of resentment and bitterness, leaving room for peace and healing.

Asking for Forgiveness

When seeking forgiveness, it is essential to be sensitive to the emotions and timeline of the hurt partner. It requires expressing genuine remorse for the actions that caused the hurt and understanding the pain that has been caused. It is important to give the hurt partner enough time to process their feelings and come to a decision about whether or not to forgive. It is vital to allow the hurt partner to feel and express their emotions without judgment or interruption. It might take time and effort to rebuild trust, and it is crucial to be patient and consistent during this process. Seeking forgiveness is a complex process that requires honesty, vulnerability, and empathy.

Strategies for Self-Forgiveness

Self-forgiveness is a crucial and often overlooked aspect of personal healing and the recovery of relationships. This process involves acknowledging one's mistakes, taking responsibility for them, and learning from them. It requires a conscious effort to release oneself from the grip of self-blame, shame, and bitterness. Self-forgiveness is an essential step in restoring self-esteem and facilitating overall relationship healing. The process requires self-compassion and self-love, as well as a willingness to recognize one's own humanity and imperfections. It involves accepting that everyone makes mistakes and that they are a natural part of the human experience.

Practicing self-forgiveness underscores the importance of empathy, patience, and a commitment to growth and healing within relationships. Effective apologies and forgiveness are critical components of this process. Couples who can understand and practice these skills can navigate the challenges of conflicts and emerge stronger. It is through self-forgiveness that one can move forward with a renewed sense of self-awareness, peace, and understanding.

Re-establishing Intimacy After Conflict

When a conflict arises in a relationship, it can cause emotional distance and weaken the bond between partners. However, it's important to understand that conflicts are an inevitable part of any relationship and taking steps to re-establish intimacy is crucial for the healing and strengthening of the relationship. This journey back to closeness requires intentional effort from both individuals, focusing on emotional, physical, and spiritual reconnection. In order to achieve this, it's necessary to address not only the immediate aftermath of the conflict but also the deeper emotional wounds that may have been inflicted or reopened. By doing this, partners can rebuild trust and repair any damage that may have been done, leading to a stronger and healthier relationship.

Conflict can have a profound impact on the intimacy between partners, causing a breakdown in communication, a reduction in affection, and a reluctance to share personal thoughts or feelings. These negative effects can gradually erode the foundation of intimacy, leading to emotional distance and disconnection. To counteract these harmful effects, it is essential to engage in open and honest communication about the hurt caused by the conflict. This involves actively listening to each other's perspectives, acknowledging and validating each other's feelings, and expressing empathy. By doing so, partners can begin to address and heal the emotional wounds caused by the conflict, restoring trust and understanding, and ultimately rebuilding their closeness.

Gradually rebuilding intimacy involves more than just resolving the conflict. Shared activities, affectionate gestures, and quality time together play a significant role in rekindling the connection. These actions demonstrate ongoing commitment and interest in each other's well-being, reinforcing the bond that exists beyond the conflict. Activities could range from simple daily routines done together, to new experiences that encourage collaboration and mutual support. Small gestures of affection, such as holding hands or leaving love notes, can also make significant strides in bringing partners closer.

After a conflict, rebuilding sexual intimacy requires sensitivity and careful navigation. While it can be a powerful way to reconnect with one's partner, it can also be a source of vulnerability and tension. Therefore, open and honest discussions about desires, boundaries, and comfort levels are crucial for rebuilding trust and ensuring that both partners feel safe and valued. To navigate this delicate area, it is recommended to take things slowly and prioritize emotional intimacy first. This can mean spending more time talking and engaging in activities that build emotional closeness before gradually reintroducing physical touch. It's important to respect each partner's needs and comfort levels throughout this process, which may involve setting boundaries and agreeing on what is and isn't okay.

Another essential tip is to focus on communication and actively listen to each other. This means being attentive to verbal and non-verbal cues and expressing oneself clearly and respectfully. It's also important to be patient and understanding, recognizing that rebuilding sexual intimacy may take time and effort. Rebuilding sexual intimacy after a conflict requires patience, communication, and a willingness to prioritize emotional closeness over physical touch initially. By taking things slowly, respecting each other's needs and comfort levels, and prioritizing open communication, couples can successfully navigate this delicate area and strengthen their bond.

In any relationship, communication plays a crucial role in building intimacy and strengthening bonds between partners. However, when intimacy is lost due to conflicts or misunderstandings, the importance of ongoing communication becomes even more critical. Regular check-ins are essential to rebuild intimacy and prevent further conflicts. By checking in with each other about their needs, fears, and comfort levels, partners can gain a better understanding of each other's perspectives and work together to address any concerns. This open dialogue offers opportunities to celebrate progress and reinforces the mutual commitment to the relationship's growth.

Through ongoing communication, partners can continue to adapt and grow together, ensuring their relationship remains strong and resilient in the face of future challenges. It's important to note that effective communication requires active listening, empathy, and a willingness to compromise. By nurturing open and honest communication, partners can create a safe and supportive environment that fosters intimacy, trust, and long-lasting love.

Setting Boundaries: The Foundation of Mutual Respect

In any relationship, setting clear and respected boundaries is essential for building trust and mutual respect. Healthy boundaries form the foundation of a healthy dynamic between partners, allowing them to feel secure and valued. These boundaries encompass various aspects of a relationship, including personal space, friendships, and interactions with family.

Personal space is an essential component of healthy boundaries. It is essential to recognize and respect each partner's need for personal space, both physical and emotional. By doing so, both partners can maintain their individuality and avoid feeling smothered or suffocated in the relationship. Friendships outside of the relationship are another aspect of healthy boundaries. It's essential to respect each other's friendships and recognize that they are an important part of their lives. Partners should avoid being overly possessive or jealous and instead encourage each other to maintain healthy friendships.

Navigating family interactions can also be a challenging aspect of a relationship. It's important to approach these interactions with sensitivity and respect. Each partner should communicate their expectations and limits when it comes to family interactions, and both should strive to honor and respect these boundaries. Defining healthy boundaries requires understanding and communicating what each partner is comfortable with in various areas of their lives. Establishing boundaries early on can prevent misunderstandings and ensure that both partners feel heard and respected. By doing so, partners can build a healthy and fulfilling relationship based on mutual trust and respect.

Effective communication and negotiation of boundaries is a vital aspect of any healthy relationship. It requires a certain level of openness, honesty, and willingness to listen to your partner's needs and concerns. The key strategies to establish and maintain boundaries in a relationship include using "I" statements to express your feelings and needs without blaming, being clear and specific about what is acceptable and what is not, and being willing to compromise and find solutions that respect both partners' boundaries.

Respecting and upholding boundaries, even when it becomes challenging, is essential for maintaining trust and respect in a relationship. It involves recognizing when it's necessary to adjust your behavior, acknowledging when you've crossed a boundary, and apologizing for your mistake. Moreover, it requires you to actively work on ensuring your actions align with the agreed-upon limits of the relationship. This can be achieved by taking the time to understand your partner's expectations, asking for clarification when needed, and continuously checking in with each other to ensure you are both on the same page. Ultimately, setting and maintaining healthy boundaries in a relationship can help foster a deeper sense of intimacy, trust, and respect between partners.As relationships grow and change, so too might the boundaries within them. Maintaining an ongoing dialogue about each partner's needs allows for adjustments to be made in a way that respects both individuals' growth and changes. This ongoing negotiation ensures that the relationship continues to be built on a foundation of mutual respect and trust, which are essential for a healthy, lasting partnership.

The Role of Physical Affection in Healing and Connection

Physical touch plays a significant role in repairing emotional rifts and strengthening the bonds of intimacy in a relationship. It serves as a bridge, reconnecting partners through the profound yet simple language of touch, which speaks directly to our most primal needs for connection and security. The healing power of physical affection lies in its ability to communicate love, forgiveness, and commitment without words, providing a tangible reassurance of the relationship's resilience and the partners' mutual care for each other. Whether it's a warm embrace, a gentle caress, or a tender kiss, physical affection has the remarkable ability to soothe our souls and ignite our passion, reminding us of the profound depth of our love and the beauty of our shared journey together.

Extensive research has shown that physical affection has a plethora of psychological and physiological benefits. These benefits include significant reduction in stress levels and an increase in bonding hormones, such as oxytocin. By engaging in regular, affectionate physical contact, such as hugging or holding hands, individuals can experience a stronger sense of emotional connection with their partners. This powerful bond serves as an antidote to the isolating effects of conflict, which can create barriers and hinder unity and trust between partners. By engaging in physical affection, couples can lower these barriers and re-establish a sense of unity and trust, leading to more fulfilling relationships. (Floyd, 2006[1]).

Incorporating physical affection in our daily interactions with our partners is an excellent way to enhance the emotional climate of a relationship. However, it takes mindfulness and a willingness to adapt to each partner's comfort levels and preferences. It's about finding those moments where physical touch can be a natural and welcome expression of love and affection. This might mean establishing new routines that include more physical closeness, such as cuddling for a few minutes before starting the day or embracing when reuniting after time apart. Creating a habit of physical touch in a relationship can help to create a deeper connection and increase intimacy. Physical touch is a powerful way to communicate love and affection, but it is essential to be aware of each partner's boundaries and comfort levels to make it a positive and enjoyable experience for both partners. According to Gulledge et al. (2003[2]), incorporating physical touch into daily interactions can help to improve the emotional climate of the relationship and foster a stronger bond between partners.

After a conflict, it is common for a couple to experience challenges in re-establishing physical closeness. This can be due to a lack of trust and feeling uncomfortable around each other. In order to overcome this, it is important to approach the process of rebuilding physical intimacy with patience and understanding. One way to do this is to start with less intimate forms of physical affection, such as holding hands or gentle hugs, and gradually increase contact as both partners begin to feel more comfortable. This gradual approach can help to rebuild trust and rekindle intimacy without overwhelming either partner. It facilitates a smoother transition back to physical closeness, allowing the couple to take their time and build a strong foundation.

It is crucial to prioritize consent and ongoing communication about physical affection. Both partners should feel comfortable with and positive about their physical interactions. This means regularly checking in with each other about what feels good and what doesn't, respecting boundaries, and being willing to adjust behaviors as needed. This open dialogue about physical affection not only strengthens the relationship but also deepens mutual understanding and respect. By focusing on patience, understanding, and communication, couples can overcome the challenges of physical intimacy after a conflict. Working together to rebuild trust and respect will not only strengthen their bond but also help them move forward in a healthy and positive way.

Conclusion

As we conclude this chapter, we've explored the critical role of re-establishing intimacy, setting boundaries, and the power of physical affection in the aftermath of conflicts. These elements are foundational to healing emotional wounds, fostering mutual respect, and securing a deepened connection between partners. We've discussed practical strategies for navigating these complex areas, emphasizing the importance of communication, patience, and empathy.

Looking ahead, Chapter 7: "Leveraging Conflicts for Personal and Relational Growth" promises to shift our perspective on conflicts from challenges to opportunities. It will delve into how couples can use conflicts as catalysts for growth, deepening understanding, and strengthening their relationship. By embracing conflicts as part of the relationship's evolution, couples can learn valuable lessons about themselves, each other, and the dynamics of their partnership, laying the groundwork for a more resilient and fulfilling future together.

Chapter Seven

Leveraging Conflict for Personal and Relational Growth

Transforming Conflicts into Opportunities for Growth

When we find ourselves in a conflict, our natural response is often discomfort and avoidance. However, a shift in perspective can allow us to approach conflicts with a growth mindset, seeing them not as obstacles to avoid but as opportunities for personal and relational development. By reframing conflicts in this way, we can move beyond our immediate discomfort and instead focus on the potential for positive change they offer.

Recognizing the inherent value in conflicts is crucial to this perspective shift. Rather than viewing them as negative experiences to be avoided, we can see them as opportunities to grow and learn. In doing so, we can begin to approach conflicts with a sense of open-minded curiosity rather than defensiveness or aggression. This shift in perspective can ultimately transform conflicts from sources of stress into catalysts for strengthening relationships. By embracing their learning and growth opportunities, we can build deeper connections with others and become more resilient and adaptable in the face of future challenges.

Post-Traumatic Growth in Relationship Conflicts

Post-traumatic growth (PTG) is a fascinating and empowering framework that helps us understand how people can become stronger and more resilient from the challenges and difficulties they experience. Originally, PTG was applied to the aftermath of traumatic events, but it can also be extended to the realm of relationship conflicts. Although relationship conflicts can be painful, they offer unique opportunities for growth and learning. By navigating through conflicts, partners can develop a deeper understanding of each other, build stronger emotional bonds, and foster greater empathy. Research has shown that adversity has transformative potential, and individuals who face their struggles head-on can experience significant personal growth and development (Tedeschi & Calhoun, 2004[1]).

Identifying Growth Opportunities in Conflict

Identifying growth opportunities during conflict is a deliberate process that requires careful thought and open communication. It involves taking the time to reflect on oneself and engaging in honest and non-defensive dialogue with others. The aim is to understand what can be learned from the experience and how relationships can be improved due to the conflict.

One of the key strategies in this process is self-reflection. By introspecting on one's own role in the conflict and identifying areas for personal growth and improvement, individuals can gain a deeper understanding of the situation and their own behavior. This can help to prevent similar conflicts from arising in the future.

Another important strategy is open dialogue. Encouraging honest and non-defensive communication about each partner's feelings, needs, and perspectives can help to build trust and mutual understanding. It can also help uncover the conflict's underlying causes and identify constructive paths forward.

By combining these approaches, individuals can gain a more nuanced understanding of conflict and its growth potential. They can identify personal and relational development opportunities and work towards more positive and constructive outcomes.

Examples of Conflict Reframing

In any relationship, conflicts are almost inevitable. It's not uncommon for disagreements to arise over issues such as finances, parenting styles, or time management. However, instead of viewing these conflicts as negative, they can be seen as opportunities for learning and growth in the relationship. For instance, let's say a couple disagrees over financial priorities. Instead of becoming angry with each other, they could use this situation as a chance to have a deeper conversation about their values and future goals. This kind of conversation can be incredibly constructive, as it fosters a sense of shared purpose and helps each partner better understand the other's perspectives. Similarly, differing parenting styles need not be a source of strife. Instead, these differences can be viewed as an opportunity to discuss family dynamics and mutual support. When parents can work together and support one another, they create a stronger sense of teamwork and cohesiveness within the family unit. Ultimately, reframing conflict in this way can help you see your partner or family member not as an opponent but as a collaborator in creating a stronger, more fulfilling relationship.

Maintaining a Positive Outlook on Growth

Maintaining a positive outlook on the growth potential, even when progress seems slow, is crucial for achieving success in any field. This mindset is about having an unwavering belief in yourself and your abilities and keeping your eyes firmly fixed on your long-term goals, even in the face of short-term setbacks. It's important to remember that progress is often incremental, and every small victory counts. Whether mastering a new skill, progressing towards a difficult project, or simply overcoming a personal obstacle, each step forward is a cause for celebration.

At the same time, it's essential to recognize that setbacks and challenges are a natural part of the process. When things don't go as planned, it can be easy to become discouraged or give up altogether. But by maintaining a positive outlook and staying focused on the bigger picture, you can cultivate the resilience and perseverance needed to overcome even the most challenging obstacles. Ultimately, success in any endeavor is about staying committed, focused, and positive. By celebrating small victories and recognizing that every effort towards understanding and compromise contributes to a stronger, more resilient relationship, you can build the foundation for a successful and fulfilling future.

Transforming conflicts into opportunities for growth not only helps resolve immediate issues but also strengthens relationships over the long term. Couples can foster a more supportive, understanding, and loving partnership by embracing conflict as an avenue for learning and improvement.

Personal Growth and Its Impact on the Relationship

Developing oneself personally is a fundamental aspect of improving the dynamics of any relationship. When individuals embark on a journey of personal growth, it positively impacts their partnership's overall health and fulfillment. Deepening the bonds between partners is a significant benefit that arises from an inward quest for self-improvement. This process involves introspection, self-awareness, and a willingness to learn and evolve continuously. It also helps individuals develop healthy habits, set realistic expectations, and communicate more effectively with their partners. Ultimately, personal development is a powerful tool that can bring partners closer, enhance their emotional bond, and foster a deeper sense of intimacy and trust.

The Benefits of Self-Awareness and Emotional Maturity

Developing self-awareness and emotional maturity through conflict resolution is essential to maintaining healthy relationships. When individuals take the time for introspection and work on their emotional intelligence, they are better equipped to handle interactions with others. Emotional intelligence allows individuals to bring greater understanding, compassion, and empathy to their relationships. This maturity, in turn, leads to more effective communication, a reduction in unnecessary conflicts, and a more supportive environment for addressing issues.

Emotional growth also fosters empathy, which is essential for partners to understand each other's perspectives and feelings better. When partners can better understand each other's perspectives, they are more likely to show mutual respect and love, even when disagreeing. This type of empathy can lead to a deeper level of intimacy and connection in the relationship.

Ultimately, investing in emotional growth and conflict resolution skills is an investment in the health and happiness of your relationship. It allows for greater understanding, a stronger connection, and a more fulfilling life with your partner (Gottman & Silver, 2015[2]).

Encouraging Each Other's Personal Growth

Encouraging and supporting each other's personal growth journeys within the context of a relationship is a crucial aspect of building a strong and healthy bond with your partner. This involves actively celebrating each other's achievements and progress, no matter how small they may be. It's important to acknowledge and appreciate your partner's effort in their personal growth and development and to let them know you recognize and value their hard work.

Providing a safe and non-judgmental space for sharing thoughts, fears, and dreams is essential. This means actively listening to your partner's concerns, offering support and guidance when needed, and refraining from criticism or judgment. Creating an atmosphere of trust and openness in your relationship is vital, where both partners feel comfortable sharing and discussing their innermost thoughts and feelings.

Furthermore, motivating each other to pursue interests and goals that foster individual fulfillment is crucial in supporting personal growth and development. Encouraging your partner to pursue their passions and interests, even if they may not align perfectly with yours, can help them achieve a sense of fulfillment and purpose. Similarly, sharing your own interests and goals with your partner can help them understand you better and foster a deeper connection in your relationship.

Overall, a supportive approach to personal growth within a relationship strengthens the bond between partners and enriches the relationship with shared experiences and new perspectives.

Balancing Individuality and Togetherness

Maintaining a healthy relationship requires striking a delicate balance between individuality and togetherness. On the one hand, personal growth is essential for improving one's well-being and enriching the relationship. On the other hand, fostering togetherness helps solidify a shared sense of identity and purpose, bringing partners closer together. A relationship that allows both partners to freely explore their interests and passions while engaging in joint activities and pursuing common goals is the key to achieving this balance. Such a dynamic ensures that each partner feels appreciated and respected as an individual while also being an integral part of a supportive and loving partnership (Kabat-Zinn & Kabat-Zinn, 2017[3]).

The Role of Self-Care and Self-Compassion

Self-care and self-compassion are two essential components of personal growth that can significantly impact the quality of relationships. Self-care involves taking the time to engage in activities that promote physical, emotional, and mental well-being. By prioritizing self-care, individuals can enhance their capacity to contribute positively to their relationships. This allows them to show up as their best selves, with more energy, patience, and resilience to navigate the ups and downs of their interactions with their partners.

Similarly, self-compassion is an attitude of kindness and understanding towards oneself. It involves recognizing and accepting one's imperfections, mistakes, and limitations without judgment or criticism. By practicing self-compassion, individuals can reduce the likelihood of projecting their insecurities, fears, or frustrations onto their partners. Instead, they can approach their relationships with a more open, loving, and forgiving mindset, fostering deeper connections, greater intimacy, and more meaningful interactions.

Self-care and self-compassion can create a positive feedback loop that strengthens the relationship over time. As individuals prioritize their physical, emotional, and mental well-being, they become more attuned to their needs and feelings, which can help them communicate more effectively with their partners. They can also model healthy behaviors and attitudes that inspire their partners to care for themselves and practice self-compassion. By creating a culture of self-care and self-compassion, couples can build a more loving, supportive, and fulfilling dynamic that benefits both partners (Neff, 2011[4]).

Fostering personal growth is a journey toward self-improvement and a path to enriching and deepening romantic relationships. By cultivating self-awareness, emotional maturity, and mutual support for each other's journeys, partners can create a more fulfilling and resilient bond that can stand the test of time.

The Power of Shared Goals and Values

When we align on shared goals and values, we create a powerful force that strengthens our relationships and brings us together. This unity provides a common direction and fosters collective growth, paving the way for deeper connection and understanding. Let us work towards this alignment, which cements partnerships and inspires us to achieve greatness.

Exercises for Identifying Shared Goals and Values

Couples who share a vision and have common goals and values are likelier to have a happy and fulfilling relationship. However, identifying and discussing these shared goals and values can be challenging. That's why introducing exercises such as shared vision boards, goal-setting sessions, and values mapping can be beneficial.

Shared vision boards visually represent the goals and values that couples want to achieve together. These boards can include images, quotes, and symbols representing their shared aspirations. Goal-setting sessions involve setting specific, measurable, achievable, relevant, and time-bound (SMART) goals aligned with the couple's shared vision. Values mapping, however, involves identifying and prioritizing the most important values to each partner and finding overlapping areas.

These activities encourage open dialogue and reflection, which can help partners to understand each other's aspirations and core values more deeply. Through this process, couples can discover common ground and develop a unified vision for their future together. This can lead to a stronger and more fulfilling relationship as they work together towards their shared goals and values.

Navigating Differences in Goals and Values

In any relationship, it's common to have differences in goals and values. These differences can arise due to our unique backgrounds, experiences, and perspectives. However, it's essential to navigate these differences respectfully and openly to maintain a healthy and happy relationship.

One of the key strategies for navigating differences in goals and values is to practice open and respectful communication. This means that both partners should be willing to listen to each other's viewpoints without judgment or criticism. By doing so, they can better understand each other's needs and perspectives, which can help them find common ground and work towards a mutually agreeable solution.

Another important strategy is to seek to understand before being understood. This means that both partners should try to understand each other's positions and perspectives before presenting their own. This can help create an environment of trust and respect where both partners feel heard and valued. When differences arise, it's essential to view them as opportunities for growth. Rather than seeing them as roadblocks, couples can use these differences to learn more about each other and create new shared aspirations that reflect a blend of both partners' desires and values. This approach fosters adaptability and resilience within the relationship, which can help it withstand challenges and difficulties over time.

Finding compromises that honor both partners' needs is critical to navigating differences in goals and values. By working together and being open to new possibilities, couples can create a fulfilling, supportive relationship built on a foundation of trust and respect.

Integrating Shared Goals and Values into Daily Life

To ensure that shared goals and values are integrated into daily life, couples can take specific steps. One of these is to have regular check-ins with each other to assess how the partnership is progressing towards these shared objectives. This not only keeps the partnership on track but also helps to maintain open communication between partners. Another way to reinforce the importance of these shared goals and values is to celebrate related milestones. This can be done by going out for a special dinner or planning a small getaway to commemorate the achievement. By acknowledging and celebrating these milestones, partners can feel a sense of accomplishment and motivation to continue working towards their shared objectives.

Lastly, making decisions that align with these common principles is essential. Whether deciding where to go on vacation or how to handle a disagreement, partners should always keep their shared goals and values in mind. This ensures that their actions and decisions align with their long-term vision for the partnership. By actively incorporating shared goals and values into their daily lives, couples can strengthen their commitment to each other and the partnership's long-term success.

Impact on Conflict Resolution

In conflict resolution, shared goals and values are essential elements that can guide individuals toward positive outcomes. Recalling these common objectives can help shift the focus from disagreements to collaboration during difficult situations. This shared foundation promotes cooperation between individuals, leading to a better understanding of each other's perspectives and enabling them to work together towards solutions that align with their mutual objectives. Ultimately, shared goals and values enhance the likelihood of reaching positive outcomes for all parties involved.

Shared goals and values have the incredible power to unite partners, creating a profound sense of connection and meaning. Through open communication and a willingness to integrate these common aspirations and beliefs, couples can build a resilient and thriving relationship based on mutual respect, understanding, and collaboration.

Cultivating a Positive Mindset Toward Conflicts

By adopting a positive mindset towards conflicts, you can transform the emotional landscape of your relationship. This can create a more supportive and understanding environment that encourages you and your significant other to view conflicts as growth opportunities and strengthen your bond.

Psychological Benefits of Positivity

Maintaining a positive outlook can have significant psychological benefits in the face of relationship challenges. Research has demonstrated that individuals who adopt a positive and optimistic attitude toward their relationships experience reduced stress levels, enhanced resilience, and greater overall relationship satisfaction.

Positivity plays a crucial role in enabling individuals to approach conflicts with a constructive attitude, which in turn helps them to focus on finding solutions rather than dwelling on problems. This approach can be particularly beneficial in situations where two individuals have differing opinions or where there are communication breakdowns. By maintaining a positive outlook and focusing on constructive solutions, individuals can better maintain healthy relationships and resolve conflicts mutually beneficially (Seligman, 2002[5]).

Techniques for Cultivating a Positive Mindset

Developing a positive mindset is crucial for maintaining a healthy relationship. This involves implementing intentional practices that promote gratitude and help reframe negative experiences in a more positive light. By adopting a positive perspective, individuals can improve communication, increase their ability to handle conflicts and build stronger connections with their partners.

One such technique is gratitude practices, where couples can regularly express appreciation for one another and the relationship. This practice can shift the focus from conflict to appreciation, leading to a more positive relationship dynamic. Another technique is reframing exercises, which involve actively reinterpreting conflicts as opportunities to learn and grow together. This encourages a more optimistic view of challenges and helps maintain a positive emotional tone in the relationship, even during disagreements.

By adopting these practices, couples can build a stronger foundation for their relationship, strengthen their bond, and promote a positive and supportive environment where they can both thrive.

Maintaining Positivity During Conflicts

In any relationship, conflicts are inevitable and can cause negative emotions to arise. However, maintaining a positive outlook during these situations is crucial to prevent negativity from overshadowing the love and respect between partners. To achieve this, several approaches can be taken. Firstly, it's essential to recognize and halt negative thought patterns that may arise during a conflict. This can involve taking a step back and reflecting upon the situation rather than immediately reacting with negative emotions. Doing so makes it easier to approach the problem with a clear and level-headed mindset.

Secondly, it's helpful to focus on the strength of the relationship rather than the immediate issue. This means reminding yourself of the positive aspects of the relationship and the reasons why you love and care for your partner. By doing so, the issue at hand can be put into perspective and approached more constructively.

Lastly, practicing empathy and understanding each other's perspectives is essential. Each person in a relationship is unique with their own thoughts, feelings, and experiences. By actively listening and trying to understand your partner's point of view, finding common ground and working towards a resolution becomes easier.

Adopting these approaches creates a supportive and positive atmosphere where conflicts can be resolved constructively. This helps to strengthen the relationship and promote continued love and respect between partners.

The Role of Humor and Light-heartedness

In times of conflict resolution, humor and light-heartedness can be potent tools for diffusing tension and fostering a positive outlook. Laughter can break the ice during heated moments, reminding partners of their bond and the happiness they have experienced together. When used respectfully and sensitively, humor can ease stress and create a more relaxed atmosphere, which in turn can open the door to more productive and less confrontational dialogue. Allowing humor to play a role in conflict resolution can lead to more effective and peaceful outcomes for all parties involved.

Developing a positive attitude towards conflicts can be a game-changer in any relationship. By choosing to focus on positivity, gratitude, and humor, couples can tackle challenges together in a more effective manner. This approach can make their bond stronger and more resilient with each obstacle they face.

Legacy of Love: Setting a Positive Example for Future Generations

Effective conflict resolution within a relationship is crucial for creating a healthy and positive partner dynamic. It also plays a significant role in setting an excellent example for future generations. How we handle conflicts can impart valuable lessons about love, respect, and growth, which can influence how children and others navigate their relationships. Therefore, it is essential to recognize the impact of our actions in shaping the legacy of love we leave behind.

The Concept of Legacy in Relationship Dynamics

The concept of legacy extends beyond the transfer of material possessions. It encompasses the emotional and behavioral patterns we pass on to future generations. In particular, how we navigate conflicts within our relationships is a model through which children and other observers learn how to manage emotions, respect differences, and communicate effectively. This transmission of values and behaviors has a profound impact on the emotional well-being and relationship skills of future generations. Therefore, it is crucial to be mindful of the legacy we are leaving behind and make a conscious effort to model positive behaviors and values in our relationships.

Modeling Healthy Conflict Resolution Strategies

As parents and caregivers, it is essential to understand that conflict is a natural part of life. However, it is equally important to model healthy conflict resolution strategies for children to equip them with the necessary tools to manage it effectively. This involves emphasizing the importance of communication, empathy, and mutual respect.

Teaching children how to listen actively, express their feelings constructively, and seek common ground can help them develop valuable life skills essential for building strong, respectful relationships. By modeling these behaviors, caregivers can help children understand the importance of emotional intelligence and conflict management.

In short, by demonstrating healthy conflict resolution strategies, caregivers can help children develop the tools to build positive relationships and navigate conflict constructively and respectfully.

Discussing Relationship Challenges with Children

When discussing relationship challenges and resolutions with children, it's crucial to follow certain guidelines to ensure that the conversations are age-appropriate and effective. One of the most important things to remember is that the discussions should emphasize the importance of understanding, forgiveness, and teamwork. By doing so, children can be reassured that conflicts are normal and can be resolved positively.

To achieve this, it's essential to approach the conversations with empathy and sensitivity, considering the child's age, temperament, and level of emotional maturity. For younger children, using simple language and concrete examples may help them understand the concepts of forgiveness and teamwork. For older children, engaging in more in-depth discussions about the nature of conflict and how it can be resolved in healthy ways may be appropriate.

Ultimately, these conversations can profoundly impact the emotional bond within the family and the child's development. By providing children with a secure foundation for their emotional growth and development, parents can help them navigate life's challenges with greater resilience and confidence.

The Long-term Benefits of Setting a Positive Example

Positive conflict resolution skills have far-reaching benefits that extend beyond the immediate situation at hand. By modeling effective conflict management, we can help develop emotional intelligence and promote healthy relationship skills that can be passed down to future generations. When children grow up observing constructive conflict resolution, they are more likely to adopt these behaviors in their relationships, creating a cycle of positive relationship dynamics that can endure across generations. This helps strengthen individual relationships and contributes to the development of stronger, healthier communities and societies as a whole.

We can leave a legacy of love that enriches our relationships and guides future generations. By approaching conflicts with love, respect, and a focus on growth, we create a valuable inheritance that offers lessons extending far beyond our own lives.

Conclusion

In this chapter, we explored the transformative power of approaching conflicts with a mindset geared toward growth, understanding, and positivity. We discussed how personal development, shared goals and values, and a positive approach to conflicts can strengthen relationships, providing practical strategies and insights for turning challenges into opportunities for deeper connection and collaboration.

Looking ahead, the next chapter, "Inclusive Perspective on Conflict Resolution," will build upon these foundations by introducing strategies for conflict resolution that respect and celebrate diversity within relationships. We will delve into how embracing an inclusive perspective can enrich relationships, fostering a deeper understanding and appreciation for the unique backgrounds, cultures, and experiences that each partner brings to the relationship.

By continuing to approach conflict with empathy, respect, and an open heart, we can lay the groundwork for relationships that are resilient in the face of adversity and deeply enriched by the diversity and complexity of human experience.

Chapter Eight

Inclusive Perspectives on Conflict Resolution

Cultural Differences and Their Impact on Conflict Resolution

Cultural backgrounds play a pivotal role in shaping individuals' approaches to conflict, influencing communication styles and resolution strategies uniquely. This diversity necessitates a deep understanding and appreciation of cultural nuances within intimate relationships to foster effective conflict resolution.

Understanding and navigating the complexities introduced by cultural differences in a relationship are not just beneficial but essential for fostering a healthy, respectful, and supportive environment. As Ting-Toomey and Oetzel (2013[1]) emphasize, culture impacts conflict management styles significantly, with variances across dimensions such as individualism vs. collectivism, direct vs. indirect communication, and the importance of saving face.

Cultural Sensitivity and Awareness

Recognizing and appreciating your partner's cultural background and its influence on their conflict resolution style are crucial. Cultural sensitivity entails more than just acknowledging differences; it involves actively learning about, respecting, and integrating these differences into the relationship's conflict resolution process. According to Chen (2020[2]), cultural awareness in relationships promotes deeper empathy and understanding, allowing couples to navigate conflicts more effectively by appreciating the underlying cultural values that shape their partner's responses.

Strategies for Bridging Cultural Gaps

Bridging cultural gaps requires open discussions about each partner's cultural values and expectations. This dialogue is not about erasing cultural identities but about creating a shared space where both partners feel seen, heard, and respected. Implementing strategies like active listening, acknowledging cultural norms, and expressing curiosity about your partner's cultural background can significantly reduce misunderstandings (LeBaron, 2003[3]).

Navigating Common Cultural Misunderstandings

Misunderstandings stemming from cultural differences can be particularly challenging. For instance, directness in communication, considered forthright and honest in some cultures, might be perceived as rude or aggressive in others. Identifying these potential flashpoints and discussing them openly can help couples find a middle ground that respects both cultures (Avruch, 1998[4]).

Creating a Blended Culture Within the Relationship

One of the most beautiful outcomes of intercultural relationships is the opportunity to create a blended culture that honors both partners' backgrounds. This involves mutual respect, compromise, and the creation of new traditions that reflect the couple's unique cultural amalgam. As Kim et al. (2008[5]) suggest, this blended cultural environment supports the growth of a strong, unified relationship identity that values diversity and inclusivity.

Recognizing and embracing cultural differences in conflict resolution can significantly enhance the depth and quality of a relationship. Through cultural sensitivity, open dialogue, and the creation of a blended culture, couples can navigate conflicts more effectively, fostering a more inclusive and understanding partnership.

Navigating Relationship Dynamics Across Different Life Stages

Evolving Relationships Through Life Stages

Relationships go through different stages as they progress, each of which introduces unique challenges and opportunities for resolving conflicts and growing together. Since relationships are dynamic, the strategies used to resolve conflicts must adapt and evolve to meet the changing needs and circumstances of the partners involved.

In the early stages of a relationship, conflicts may arise from understanding and negotiating personal boundaries, aligning future goals, and integrating lives. As relationships mature, the nature of conflicts tends to shift, reflecting deeper issues such as financial management, parenting, and balancing career aspirations. Understanding these patterns of development is crucial for maintaining a healthy relationship over time (Gottman & Silver, 1999[6]).

Adjusting to Major Life Transitions

Going through major life changes, such as starting a family, switching career paths, or retiring, is never easy. These transitions can bring about various challenges and uncertainties that can seriously impact the dynamics of a relationship. If not handled with care and consideration, they can even lead to conflicts and push partners apart. However, by adopting adaptive strategies and working together to find joint solutions, couples can navigate these transitions with more ease. Embracing change as an opportunity for growth can also help partners maintain a positive outlook and come out stronger on the other side (Parker, 2013[7]).

Maintaining Connection and Understanding Over Time

As relationships progress over time, it is important for partners to actively work on maintaining a strong connection with each other. This can be achieved through regular check-ins, shared activities, and open communication about individual needs and desires. These practices can serve as powerful tools to reinforce the bond between partners, especially during periods of change or growth. By setting aside time to engage in meaningful conversations and activities, partners can deepen their understanding of each other and build a foundation of trust, respect, and mutual support. This can help them navigate the challenges and transitions that are an inevitable part of any long-term relationship (Johnson, 2008[8]).

The Role of Flexibility and Communication

Successful relationships require a strong foundation built on flexibility and open communication. The ever-changing landscape of a relationship demands that both partners remain open to change, willing to adapt, and committed to transparently discussing each other's evolving needs and expectations. This means that managing conflicts and fostering growth at any stage of a relationship requires a deep understanding of how to embrace these principles.

By being flexible, partners can navigate the twists and turns that inevitably arise in any relationship. This means being open to suggestions and new ideas, being willing to compromise, and being ready to adjust plans and expectations as needed. Open communication is also essential, as it allows partners to share their thoughts, feelings, and concerns in a safe and supportive environment. This fosters mutual understanding, empathy, and respect, all of which are essential elements in building a strong and healthy relationship.

When conflicts do arise, partners who are committed to flexibility and open communication are better equipped to navigate them successfully. They can work together to find solutions that meet both partners' needs and expectations, rather than focusing on "winning" the argument or getting their way. This creates a sense of teamwork and trust, which is essential in fostering growth and strengthening the relationship over time. In short, embracing flexibility and open communication can transform challenges into opportunities for strengthening the relationship. By being open to change, willing to adapt, and committed to transparently discussing each other's evolving needs and expectations, partners can build a strong foundation that will stand the test of time (Gottman et al., 2010[9]).

Recognizing and embracing the evolving nature of relationship dynamics across different life stages is crucial for conflict resolution and growth. By acknowledging the unique challenges and opportunities each stage presents, and focusing on flexibility, communication, and connection, partners can navigate these transitions together, creating a resilient and enduring partnership that can stand the test of time.

LGBTQ+ Relationships: Unique Challenges and Strategies

Understanding the Unique Landscape

Navigating relationships within the LGBTQ+ community can be a complex journey. Societal and familial pressures can create a challenging landscape for LGBTQ+ couples, who may face unique difficulties in their relationships. Internal struggles with identity, self-acceptance, and mental health can also add additional layers of complexity to these dynamics. These challenges can significantly impact conflict resolution in LGBTQ+ relationships, making it important to develop tailored strategies that take into account the unique experiences and needs of each individual.

Facing External Judgment and Internalized Stigma

LGBTQ+ couples face a range of external judgments due to societal norms and prejudices, which can have a significant impact on their relationship. These external pressures can be compounded by internalized stigma, leading to negative effects on an individual's self-esteem and overall relationship dynamic. In order to foster a healthy and fulfilling relationship, it is essential to recognize and confront these external and internal pressures. By doing so, individuals can work towards building a relationship that is grounded in mutual respect, love, and understanding, free from the influence of external societal pressures and internalized stigma (Meyer, 2003[10]).

Tailored Strategies for Conflict Resolution

Navigating conflicts in LGBTQ+ relationships can be complex, as these partnerships often face unique pressures due to societal attitudes and internalized stigma. To address these challenges, it is important to develop customized strategies that take into account the specific context of each relationship. Open communication between partners is crucial in order to discuss the impact of societal attitudes and foster mutual understanding. By actively challenging internalized stigma and employing affirming communication techniques, partners can support each other and strengthen their relationship against these unique challenges. It is important to acknowledge the complexity of LGBTQ+ relationships and to approach conflict resolution with care, empathy, and a commitment to creating a safe and supportive environment for both partners (Herek, 2009[11]).

Building a Strong Support System

In today's society, being a part of the LGBTQ+ community can often come with various challenges and obstacles. Therefore, it is essential to have a robust support system to navigate through these difficulties. Building a support network within the relationship and outside of it can be of immense help in developing resilience and coping mechanisms. This network can consist of close friends, family members who are allies, LGBTQ+ community resources, and professional counseling services that cater specifically to the needs of the LGBTQ+ community. With this support system in place, individuals can better manage external stressors, receive affirmation and encouragement, and draw strength from a community that understands and accepts them for who they are (Pachankis, 2014[12]).

Resources and Community Connection

For LGBTQ+ couples who may face unique challenges in their relationships, there are numerous resources available that can provide additional support, guidance, counseling, and a sense of belonging. These resources include LGBTQ+ advocacy organizations, support groups, and specialized therapists who are knowledgeable about the specific issues that LGBTQ+ couples may encounter. By engaging with these resources, LGBTQ+ couples can gain valuable tools and insights for navigating relationship challenges, such as communication issues, conflicts around identity or family acceptance, and navigating the legal and social systems that can impact their relationships. In addition, these resources provide opportunities for connecting with others who share similar experiences, which can foster a sense of community and solidarity.

LGBTQ+ advocacy organizations offer a range of services, from legal support and advocacy to community engagement and education. Many of these organizations also provide resources specifically for LGBTQ+ couples, such as relationship workshops, counseling services, and social events. Support groups can offer a safe and confidential space for LGBTQ+ couples to connect with others who understand their experiences and offer support and encouragement. Specialized therapists who have experience working with LGBTQ+ couples can provide targeted and effective support for relationship issues. These therapists can help couples navigate challenges related to societal stigma, family dynamics, and communication issues, among other concerns. They can also offer guidance and support in navigating the legal and social systems that can impact their relationships, such as adoption or marriage laws.

Overall, these resources can provide LGBTQ+ couples with the support, guidance, and sense of community they need to navigate the unique challenges they may face in their relationships. By taking advantage of these resources, LGBTQ+ couples can build stronger, healthier relationships and create a brighter future for themselves and their communities. (GLSEN, 2020[13]).

LGBTQ+ couples can overcome unique challenges and strengthen their relationships by using targeted resources, building strong support systems, and developing effective conflict resolution strategies. With resilience, understanding, and growth, they can create a brighter future for themselves and their loved ones.

The Role of Gender in Conflict Dynamics and Resolution

Impact of Traditional Gender Roles

The impact of gender norms and expectations on conflict dynamics cannot be overstated. These cultural and societal expectations have a profound influence on how conflicts are expressed and resolved. Traditional gender roles tend to dictate communication styles and approaches to conflict, which can limit the ability of individuals to navigate disagreements effectively and authentically.

For instance, traditional gender roles can pigeonhole individuals into specific modes of communication and conflict resolution. Men are often expected to maintain stoicism in the face of adversity, which can hinder the open expression of vulnerabilities. As a result, men may struggle to communicate their feelings and needs effectively, leading to misunderstandings or unresolved conflicts. On the other hand, women may be socialized to prioritize harmony over direct conflict. This can mean that they suppress genuine concerns or grievances in order to avoid upsetting others, even if it means sacrificing their own needs or desires. This can also lead to misunderstandings or unresolved conflicts, as women may struggle to assert themselves in a way that feels true to their authentic selves.

These gender norms can have a particularly significant impact on interpersonal relationships, where communication and conflict resolution are essential to building trust and intimacy. By recognizing the impact of traditional gender roles on our communication styles and conflict resolution strategies, we can begin to challenge these norms and create more authentic and effective ways of engaging with one another (Wood & Dibble, 2015[14]).

Challenging Limiting Gender Norms

In order to overcome the limitations imposed by rigid gender norms, it is important to create an atmosphere where both partners feel comfortable expressing their emotions and needs freely. To achieve this, it is necessary to encourage open dialogue that challenges the traditional gender expectations, leading to more equitable approaches to resolving conflicts. By engaging in conversations that delve into how gender norms shape individual behavior and perceptions, we can take the critical first step towards comprehending and addressing the underlying causes of many conflicts. By fostering an environment that is conducive to open communication and breaking down gender stereotypes, we can build healthier, more fulfilling relationships that promote mutual respect and understanding (Johnson, 2017[15]).

Supporting Emotional Expression

One of the key elements of building a healthy and fulfilling relationship is creating a safe space where both partners can express themselves freely. However, due to societal gender norms and expectations, many individuals may feel pressure to suppress their emotions and needs. This can lead to misunderstandings, resentment, and ultimately, a lack of authentic connection. To combat this, it's important to actively encourage and validate emotional expression, regardless of gender. This means creating an environment where both partners feel comfortable sharing their feelings, fears, and desires without fear of judgement or rejection. By doing so, we can dismantle harmful stereotypes and foster a deeper, more authentic connection.

It's also important to acknowledge the ways in which gender roles can limit our experiences and perspectives. By demonstrating empathy and understanding towards each other's struggles with these constraints, we can build a foundation of trust and respect that strengthens the relationship. Ultimately, creating space for emotional expression and breaking down gendered expectations can lead to a more fulfilling and satisfying partnership (Carver, 2014[16]).

Embracing a Full Range of Emotional Expression

The significance of embracing a diverse range of emotional expressions and communication styles regardless of gender cannot be overstated. By moving beyond traditional gender norms, we can foster a more inclusive and supportive environment that values individuality and encourages authentic self-expression. One of the key benefits of recognizing and valuing emotional vulnerability as a strength rather than a weakness is the positive impact it can have on conflict resolution processes. Instead of suppressing emotions or resorting to defensive tactics, individuals are empowered to openly and honestly communicate their feelings and needs. This can lead to more effective and enriching conflict resolution, as both parties are better able to understand and empathize with each other's perspectives.

Overall, embracing emotional diversity and vulnerability has the potential to transform our personal and professional relationships, promoting greater understanding, compassion, and mutual respect. By prioritizing these values, we can build a more equitable and harmonious society where everyone is free to express themselves fully and authentically (Kilmartin & Smiler, 2015[17]).

When we challenge traditional gender norms and expectations, we open ourselves up to a world of possibilities. By embracing a full range of emotions and needs, we can break free from limiting stereotypes and cultivate stronger, more authentic relationships. With this mindset, we can overcome conflict more effectively and communicate with greater clarity and understanding.

Cross-Cultural Relationships: Blending and Respecting Differences

Navigating the Rich Tapestry of Differences

Cross-cultural relationships can be a wonderful opportunity for individuals to learn and appreciate a variety of cultural differences. These relationships allow partners to explore and embrace diverse traditions, values, and communication styles, which can significantly enhance the depth and resilience of their relationship. The exchange of cultural knowledge and experiences can lead to a deeper understanding and respect for each other's beliefs and backgrounds, promoting mutual growth and personal development. By acknowledging and celebrating each other's differences, cross-cultural relationships can create a unique fusion of cultures, making it one of the most enriching and rewarding experiences one can have.

The Joys and Challenges of Cross-Cultural Relationships

Cross-cultural relationships are a fascinating blend of different traditions, communication styles, and worldviews. On one hand, these relationships can be a source of great joy and excitement as partners learn about each other's cultural heritage and merge them together. The experience of blending traditions can be a great bonding experience that brings partners closer together. On the other hand, cultural differences can pose unique challenges that require careful navigation. Communication styles, for example, can vary greatly between cultures and lead to misunderstandings if not approached with sensitivity and understanding. It's important for partners in cross-cultural relationships to approach their differences with an open mind and a willingness to learn from each other. With the right attitude and approach, these relationships can be a rich source of personal growth and fulfillment (Chen, 2020[18]).

Celebrating and Integrating Cultural Backgrounds

When partners come from different cultural backgrounds, it can be a wonderful opportunity to learn and appreciate each other's heritage. Celebrating and integrating each partner's cultural background into the fabric of the relationship can be achieved through several strategies. Firstly, creating new traditions that honor both cultures is a great way to start. For example, partners can celebrate important holidays from each other's cultures, or blend elements of both cultures into their wedding ceremony.

Secondly, learning each other's languages can also be a rewarding experience. It not only helps with communication but also shows respect for each other's culture. Even if partners do not become fluent in each other's languages, learning key phrases and expressions can go a long way in fostering a deeper connection.

Finally, engaging in cultural exchange activities is another great way to integrate each other's cultural background. This can include cooking traditional dishes together, attending cultural events, visiting historical sites, or even traveling to each other's home country.

Overall, these efforts not only deepen the partners' connection but also promote a greater understanding and appreciation of each other's heritage. It is important to remember that incorporating each other's culture into the relationship should be done with open-mindedness and respect for each other's beliefs and traditions (LeBaron, 2003[19]).

Handling Conflicts Arising from Cultural Misunderstandings

When cultural misunderstandings or differing values create conflicts, resolving them requires a combination of patience, empathy, and effective communication. For couples to navigate these challenges successfully, they need to adopt a mindset of active listening and seek to understand each other's perspectives before being understood. This approach fosters mutual respect and empathy, which are crucial in finding common ground and resolving differences.

It's important to recognize that cultural norms and values can shape how each partner approaches conflict resolution. Therefore, it's essential to identify and respect each partner's cultural background and values. Couples can achieve this by actively learning about each other's cultural practices, beliefs, and values. By doing so, they can develop a deeper understanding of each other's perspectives and avoid misunderstandings or conflicts that may arise due to cultural differences.

In summary, handling conflicts that arise from cultural misunderstandings or differing values requires a proactive approach that prioritizes empathy, patience, and effective communication. By actively listening to each other's perspectives and developing conflict resolution strategies that respect both partners' cultural norms and values, couples can strengthen their relationship and build a foundation of mutual respect (Ting-Toomey & Oetzel, 2013[20]).

The Importance of Mutual Respect, Curiosity, and Openness

In order to establish a healthy and fruitful cross-cultural relationship, it is essential to cultivate mutual respect, curiosity, and a willingness to learn from and appreciate each other's cultures. By embracing each other's backgrounds with an open heart and mind, partners can effectively navigate cultural differences, building a stronger, more understanding relationship that thrives on diversity. This means taking the time to learn about each other's traditions, customs, and beliefs, and being open to discussing and exploring them together. It also means being mindful of potential cultural misunderstandings or miscommunications, and approaching them with patience, empathy, and a desire to learn and grow.

Ultimately, a successful cross-cultural relationship is one in which both partners feel valued, respected, and understood, and are able to celebrate their differences while also finding common ground and shared experiences. By committing to ongoing learning and growth, and embracing each other's unique cultural perspectives, partners can build a relationship that is rich, rewarding, and fulfilling for both parties (Kim et al., 2008[21]).

In today's increasingly globalized world, cross-cultural relationships are becoming more common. Such relationships offer a unique opportunity to explore and blend cultural differences in a way that enriches both partners' lives. By acknowledging and celebrating these differences, couples can learn from each other and grow as individuals. Integrating cultural backgrounds can be a challenge, but it is an essential aspect of building a healthy and fulfilling relationship. It is important to understand each other's cultural norms, values, and beliefs to avoid misunderstandings and conflicts. Couples can start by sharing their cultural experiences, participating in cultural events and activities, and learning each other's language. These strategies can help create a sense of unity and belonging, which is crucial for building a strong and lasting relationship.

Approaching conflicts with empathy and understanding is also vital for the success of cross-cultural relationships. It is essential to recognize that cultural differences can sometimes lead to misunderstandings and disagreements. Instead of trying to impose one's cultural values on the other, couples should try to understand each other's perspective and find a compromise that respects both cultures. This approach can help build mutual trust and respect, which are the foundations of a healthy and successful relationship.

Cross-cultural relationships can be challenging, but they also offer a unique opportunity for personal growth and cultural enrichment. By celebrating diversity, integrating cultural backgrounds, and approaching conflicts with empathy and understanding, couples can build a relationship that respects and honors the richness of their diverse heritages.

Conclusion

This chapter explored the nuanced dynamics of conflict resolution across various contexts, emphasizing the importance of cultural sensitivity, acknowledging different life stages, addressing unique challenges in LGBTQ+ relationships, and understanding the influence of gender norms. Key takeaways include the necessity for empathy, open communication, and flexibility to navigate conflicts effectively. Looking ahead, the next chapter, "Addressing Specific Conflicts," will delve into practical strategies and tools for resolving common conflicts, providing readers with actionable steps to enhance their conflict resolution skills in more specific scenarios.

Chapter Nine

Addressing Specific Conflicts

Financial Disagreements: Finding Common Ground

Understanding the Impact of Financial Stress

It is no secret that financial disagreements are a common cause of conflict in romantic relationships. Whether it's due to differing spending habits, income disparities, or clashing financial priorities, money problems can significantly strain a partnership. That's why couples must engage in clear communication, mutual understanding, and compromise to resolve financial issues and prevent them from escalating into something more significant.

Open and transparent financial conversations mitigate stress and foster a healthier relationship. It's essential to share your financial goals, concerns, and expectations with your partner and listen carefully to their perspective. By doing so, you can work together to create a financial plan that aligns with your values and needs and avoid misunderstandings and arguments down the line.

In conclusion, while financial disagreements are an inevitable part of any relationship, they don't have to be a source of constant stress and tension. By approaching these issues with openness, honesty, and a willingness to compromise, couples can work through their differences and build a stronger, more resilient partnership (Dew, 2008[1]).

Crafting a Shared Financial Vision

When managing finances in a relationship, developing a shared financial vision that aligns with both partners' values and goals is essential. This involves having open and honest discussions about each partner's aspirations and finding common ground to create a financial plan that respects both perspectives. Jointly setting financial goals ensures that both partners feel invested in the relationship's economic well-being, providing a sense of shared responsibility for the financial decisions that impact their lives. By working together to create a comprehensive financial plan, couples can establish a solid foundation for their financial future and better navigate the challenges of managing money as a team (Britt et al., 2010[2]).

Navigating Financial Disagreements

Managing finances can be a source of tension in many relationships. To avoid conflicts, it is essential to negotiate financial disagreements effectively. One way to do this is by creating a budget that accounts for all expenses, including bills, savings, and discretionary spending. It is also vital to prioritize expenses by identifying which are essential and which can be cut back on if necessary. Another strategy for effective negotiation is to engage in open and constructive dialogue with your partner. Understanding each other's spending habits and financial priorities can help you approach financial management from a balanced and unified perspective. By communicating honestly and respectfully with one another, you can work together to make informed decisions about allocating resources and achieving your shared financial objectives.

Compromise is a critical component of successful financial negotiation. Both partners should be willing to make concessions and meet each other halfway to find a solution that works for everyone involved. This could include adjusting spending habits, increasing income, or exploring new investment opportunities. By working together and being flexible, you can build a solid foundation for a financially secure future (Falke, 2012[3]).

The Role of Financial Planning

Effective financial planning can be a vital tool to avoid future conflicts and build a strong foundation for a secure future as a couple. Engaging in proactive conversations about financial goals, savings, and investment strategies can go a long way in minimizing misunderstandings and establishing clear expectations. By regularly reviewing and adjusting their financial plans, couples can ensure that their goals remain aligned with their evolving relationship and financial situation. These financial check-ins can be an opportunity to track progress, identify potential challenges, and make necessary adjustments to their plan to ensure long-term stability. Developing a comprehensive financial plan can help couples achieve their shared goals and build a strong and prosperous future together (Archuleta et al., 2011[4]).

When managing finances in a relationship, disagreements can arise due to differences in financial priorities, habits, or goals. However, navigating these disagreements requires a couple to communicate openly and honestly, actively listen to each other's perspectives, and work towards finding common ground. This may involve creating a shared financial vision that aligns with both partners' values and goals, as well as implementing practical strategies to achieve those goals. By taking a proactive approach to financial planning and working together to overcome monetary challenges, couples can strengthen their partnership and build a more secure financial future.

Parenting Conflicts: United Fronts and Diverse Approaches

Navigating Parenting Differences

Parenting can be a challenging and rewarding experience, but it can also be a source of conflict for many families. One common cause of conflict is the differences in parenting philosophies, values, and approaches between parents. For instance, one parent may be more strict, while the other is more lenient. This can lead to arguments over discipline, parenting styles, and the general upbringing of children.

Parents must collaborate to establish a consistent approach to parenting that considers each parent's values and preferences. Open communication and mutual respect are vital to resolving disagreements and ensuring that both parents are on the same page. When parents have different approaches to parenting, it can significantly affect the family dynamic. Children may feel confused and unsure of what is expected, leading to disruptive behavior and emotional turmoil. Therefore, it is essential to present a united front and demonstrate a unified approach to parenting, even if individual differences remain.

Parenting is a complex process that requires patience, understanding, and a willingness to compromise. By working together and establishing a consistent approach, parents can ensure their children receive the guidance and support they need to become happy, healthy, and well-adjusted adults (Cummings et al., 2014[5]).

Aligning on Core Values

One of the most critical aspects of successful parenting is being on the same page as your partner regarding your core values and beliefs. However, it's not uncommon for parents to have different approaches to raising children. In such cases, it's essential to have open discussions about each parent's beliefs and find common ground on fundamental principles. This will ensure that, even when methods vary, the underlying values guiding parenting decisions remain consistent.

Parents can start by identifying their core parenting values to achieve this alignment. These may include beliefs about discipline, education, religion, or other vital issues. Once these values are identified, parents can discuss how they approach each other and look for areas of overlap. For example, one parent may believe in a more authoritarian parenting style, while the other may prefer a more democratic approach. However, both parents may still agree on the importance of respect and kindness in their interactions with their children. In cases where there is significant disagreement, compromise is vital. Parents can work together to find solutions that honor their beliefs while ensuring that their children receive consistent guidance. This may involve trying different approaches and reassessing what works best for their family.

Ultimately, the goal is to create a cohesive parenting approach grounded in shared values. This will help ensure that children receive consistent guidance and support as they grow and develop (Feinberg, 2003[6]).

Presenting a United Front

Maintaining a united front is a fundamental aspect of parenting, especially when dealing with parental disagreements. It is essential to remember that while parents may have different perspectives on various issues, they must present a cohesive stance when making decisions and setting rules in front of their children. This approach can help to reinforce a sense of security and stability in children, as they are less likely to feel conflicted or confused about what is expected of them. It can also help to prevent situations where children may try to manipulate one parent against the other. By presenting a united front, parents can demonstrate to their children that they are a team, working together to ensure their well-being and promote healthy family dynamics (McHale et al., 2002[7]).

Importance of Communication and Flexibility

Effective parenting strategies require ongoing communication and flexibility to adapt to the changing needs of children as they grow and develop. As children reach different stages of life, their needs and behaviors change, and parents must adjust their parenting approach accordingly. This requires regular discussions and evaluations of parenting methods to ensure they are still effective. By revisiting these conversations, parents can identify areas that need improvement or modification, ensuring that their parenting style remains relevant to their child's needs. This approach also helps parents maintain a strong partnership in navigating the challenges of raising children and fosters a positive and nurturing environment for their children to grow and thrive (Simons et al., 2001[8]).

Parenting conflicts can be challenging, but they can be effectively managed with understanding, communication, and a commitment to presenting a united front. Parents can create a positive family environment where love and growth thrive by focusing on core values, respecting diverse approaches, and adapting strategies over time.

Intimacy Issues: Rekindling the Flame Post-Conflict

Addressing the Impact of Conflict on Intimacy

When conflicts arise within a relationship, they can cause a significant strain on the intimacy between partners. Taking intentional steps towards rekindling and reconnecting emotionally and physically becomes crucial. If left unaddressed, conflicts can continue to fester and erode the trust and connection between partners, leading to further issues down the line.

Therefore, addressing the underlying issues causing the conflict is the first and most important step towards restoring the intimacy in the relationship. By identifying the root cause of the conflict and working towards resolving it, partners can rebuild their trust, deepen their emotional connection, and strengthen their physical bond (Gottman & Silver, 1999[9]).

Rebuilding Intimacy Through Affection and Quality Time

Rebuilding intimacy in a relationship is a gradual process that requires patience and effort from both partners. One of the most effective ways to achieve this is through affectionate touch, such as holding hands, hugging, or cuddling. These physical expressions of love can help to reignite the spark between you and your partner and foster a renewed sense of closeness. Another critical aspect of rebuilding intimacy is spending quality time together. This means carving out time in your busy schedules to engage in activities that you both enjoy. Whether going for a walk, watching a movie, or cooking a meal together, these shared experiences can help to strengthen your bond and deepen your connection.

Finally, open dialogue about your desires and boundaries is crucial for rebuilding intimacy. This means being honest and vulnerable with your partner about your needs, fears, and concerns. By communicating openly and respectfully, you can create a safe space for both of you to express your feelings and work together to overcome obstacles to a deeper, more fulfilling connection (Johnson, 2008[10]).

Navigating Sensitivities and Rebuilding Trust

When rebuilding trust in the intimate aspect of a relationship, it's crucial to handle sensitivities with care and understanding. This process requires a great deal of patience and effort from both partners, as rebuilding intimacy is not an overnight task. Partners must be willing to put in the time and effort required and approach the process with a mutual commitment to rebuilding trust and intimacy. By doing so, they can gradually restore the trust and connection that may have been lost and strengthen their relationship over time (Schnarch, 2009[11]).

The Role of Vulnerability and Patience

When trying to re-establish a fulfilling, intimate connection with your partner, it's important to remember that vulnerability and patience are key. This means allowing yourself to be open and honest about your feelings and emotions, even if it feels uncomfortable or scary. It also means giving your partner the space and time to express their feelings and thoughts. You can build a stronger and more resilient relationship by creating a safe and non-judgmental space for both partners to be vulnerable and honest. This can lead to deeper levels of intimacy, trust, and understanding between you and your partner. So, don't be afraid to let your guard down and show your true self - it might be the key to a happier and more fulfilling relationship! (Perel, 2017[12]).

Overcoming intimacy issues post-conflict requires addressing underlying problems, gradually rebuilding closeness through affection and quality time, navigating sensitivities with care, and embracing vulnerability and patience. This intentional effort can rekindle the relationship's flame, enhancing physical and emotional intimacy. I find this such an important topic that it is the subject of my book "Rekindling Desire: A Couple's Guide to Rediscovering Passion Through Mindfulness and Emotional Connection[13]," published in early 2024; you can find the details in the endnote.

Balancing Work and Relationship: Striking the Right Chord

Managing Work-Related Stress

Maintaining a healthy balance between one's work demands and relationship needs can be a challenging task. It requires establishing clear boundaries, setting priorities, and providing mutual support. Failure to manage work-related stress appropriately can adversely affect the relationship dynamic. Therefore, it is crucial to address these challenges head-on and take necessary steps to ensure that professional pressures do not undermine the foundation of the relationship. By communicating openly, setting realistic expectations, and showing empathy toward one another's needs, couples can overcome these challenges and build a stronger, more resilient relationship. Remember that a supportive and nurturing relationship can help alleviate work-related stress and ultimately lead to a more fulfilling personal and professional life (Greenhaus & Beutell, 1985[14]).

Setting Healthy Work Boundaries

Creating and enforcing healthy boundaries around work is crucial to maintaining a healthy work-life balance. Unplugging from work during shared time is essential to ensure that both partners can interact well without interruptions or distractions. This means setting aside time where work discussions or activities are off-limits and prioritizing the couple's personal space and time. Establishing specific zones where work-related activities are not permitted, such as the bedroom or the dining table, is also essential. By doing so, couples can maintain a healthy relationship while still fulfilling their professional obligations (Kreiner et al., 2009[15]).

Supporting Each Other's Career Goals

When striving for individual career success, it's crucial to ensure that the importance of the relationship is not sidelined. It's equally important to support each other's professional growth and aspirations and maintain open communication. Striking a balance between personal and professional goals and prioritizing the relationship requires much effort, mutual encouragement, and understanding. Each partner should be willing to listen to the other's goals, aspirations, and concerns and work together to find a solution that works best for both. This way, both partners can achieve their dreams and goals while ensuring a healthy and thriving relationship (Russo et al., 2016[16]).

Importance of Regular Check-ins

Frequent check-ins are vital in evaluating and adapting the balance between work and personal life. Open and honest conversations allow both parties to express their needs, concerns, and suggestions. This ongoing communication ensures both individuals feel valued and supported, leading to a healthy and harmonious relationship. Regular check-ins help identify any issues or imbalances early on, allowing for quick resolution and adjustment. These discussions also promote a sense of trust and mutual respect, creating a positive work environment that benefits everyone involved. In conclusion, regular check-ins are crucial to maintaining a healthy equilibrium between professional and personal life. Everyone should prioritize them to ensure a successful and fulfilling work-life balance (Clark, 2000[17]).

Dealing with External Stressors: In-Laws, Friends, and Work

Navigating External Relationships

It's important to recognize that external stressors have the potential to impact a couple's relationship significantly. These stressors may arise from various sources, such as dynamics with in-laws, friends, or work. It is essential to have open, honest communication with your partner to navigate these relationships carefully. One of the most effective ways to maintain a healthy partnership is by setting clear boundaries and expectations with external parties. In doing so, you can work together to mitigate any potential negative impacts on your relationship and build a strong, resilient bond that can withstand external pressures.

Presenting a United Front

The influence of relationships with in-laws and friends on the couple's dynamic cannot be overstated. These external relationships can significantly impact the couple's overall happiness and well-being. Therefore, couples must present a united front when dealing with these external relationships. By doing so, they can maintain their privacy and autonomy, ensuring that these external influences do not interfere with their harmony. For example, when there is a conflict between the couple and their in-laws or friends, presenting a united front can help avoid taking sides and creating further tension. This can also help establish boundaries, protecting the couple's relationship from unwanted interference. On the other hand, if the couple fails to present a united front, it can lead to a loss of trust and respect between them, ultimately leading to a breakdown of their relationship.

Therefore, couples need to prioritize their unity and work together to navigate external relationships in a way that strengthens their bond. Doing so can create a strong foundation for their relationship, which can withstand any external challenges.

Setting Boundaries with In-Laws and Friends

Strategizing is vital when it comes to boundary negotiation with in-laws and friends. It's essential to strike a balance that acknowledges the value of these relationships while still respecting the couple's privacy and autonomy. This means setting clear boundaries around topics that are off-limits or sensitive and establishing expectations for how often and in what ways these individuals can be involved in the couple's decision-making processes. Effective boundary negotiation can help prevent conflicts and ensure everyone feels heard and respected.

Managing Work-Related Stress

Work-related stress can take a toll on individuals and their personal relationships. Therefore, developing strategies to prevent work-related stress from seeping into private life is essential. One practical approach is to establish clear boundaries between work and home life. This can be achieved by setting specific work hours and sticking to them as much as possible. It is also important to prioritize self-care, such as taking breaks throughout the workday and engaging in activities to promote relaxation and reduce stress. Additionally, maintaining open and honest communication with loved ones about work-related stress can help prevent it from negatively impacting personal relationships. By taking these proactive steps, individuals can reduce the likelihood of work-related stress spilling over into their personal lives and maintain a healthy work-life balance.

Teamwork Against External Stressors

When external stressors start to weigh down on a couple, it can significantly impact their relationship. However, addressing and mitigating these stressors can be a powerful way to reinforce their bond. By working together as a team, partners can navigate these challenges more effectively and better understand each other's needs and concerns. This can lead to a stronger and more resilient relationship, one better equipped to handle the ups and downs of life. Whether it's financial stress, family conflicts, or other external pressures, tackling these issues as a couple can help to build a stronger foundation for the future.

Conclusion

This chapter has explored strategies for managing and resolving conflicts within relationships, emphasizing the importance of understanding, communication, and flexibility across various contexts. From navigating cultural differences to addressing financial disagreements, parenting challenges, and external stressors, the key takeaway is the necessity of collaboration and empathy in fostering a healthy, resilient partnership. The book's conclusion will reflect on the journey of conflict resolution, emphasizing growth, deeper understanding, and strengthened bonds as central themes. It will encourage you to apply these insights, fostering lasting relationship improvements.

Conclusion

As we draw this book to a close, we revisit its core mission: to arm you, the reader, with practical strategies that transform relationship conflicts into gateways for growth, understanding, and deeper intimacy. This journey through the pages has underscored the foundational pillars of effective conflict resolution, weaving through the nuances of communication techniques, emotional intelligence, regulation, and frameworks that rebuild trust and intimacy. Each chapter has been a step towards leveraging conflicts not as divisions but as milestones for personal and relational evolution.

We've delved into the critical role of empathy and understanding, stressing that the ability to walk in your partner's shoes is indispensable in navigating the complexities of conflicts. Such empathy fosters a supportive, loving relationship environment where both partners feel seen and heard. Coupled with a positive mindset, this empathy transforms conflicts from potentially destructive forces into catalysts for strengthening bonds and enhancing mutual understanding.

The discourse on inclusivity and diversity within relationships has been particularly enlightening, presenting how diverse perspectives and experiences enrich conflict resolution approaches. This inclusivity ensures that our strategies are respectful and effective across the spectrum of relationships, celebrating the unique challenges and triumphs each partnership may face.

As you stand on the threshold of applying these insights to your own relationships, remember that the journey towards enhanced conflict resolution and deeper intimacy starts with a willingness to embrace change and growth. This path is not without its challenges, but the principles and practices shared in these pages aim to guide you towards a more fulfilling, harmonious, and resilient partnership.

In inviting you to share your journey and successes, we foster a community of mutual support and learning. Your dedication to improving your relationship dynamics is a profound testament to your commitment to your partner and the health of your relationship.

As we part ways, let's remember the words of Garth Brooks: "The greatest conflicts are not between two people but between one person and themselves." This powerful reminder serves as our concluding thought, motivating and inspiring hope as you turn the final page. Your journey towards understanding, empathy, and intimacy begins within, and it's a path worth embarking on for the promise of a stronger, more connected partnership.

Keeping the Game Alive

Armed with new strategies to transform relationship conflicts into moments of connection, it's your turn to pass the torch. Your insights on "Relationship Conflict Resolution" can light the way for others on their journey towards stronger, more intimate partnerships.

By sharing your honest thoughts in a review, you guide fellow seekers to the wisdom they need. Each word of your experience contributes to a larger conversation, a community dedicated to turning conflict into closeness.

Thank you for joining in the dance of giving knowledge. With your help, the art of relationship harmony spreads further.

https://geni.us/XdA6Yh

Your sharing keeps the flame of understanding burning bright, and together, we keep the game of love and connection vibrant and alive.

Endnotes

Conflict Resolution Frameworks

1. Gottman, J.M., & Silver, N. (2015). *The Seven Principles for Making Marriage Work: A Practical Guide from the Country's Foremost Relationship Expert*. New York: Harmony Books.

2. Johnson, S. (2008). *Hold Me Tight: Seven Conversations for a Lifetime of Love*. New York: Little, Brown Spark.

3. Fisher, R., Ury, W., & Patton, B. (2011). *Getting to Yes: Negotiating Agreement Without Giving In*. New York: Penguin Books.

4. Gottman, J.M., & Silver, N. (2015). *The Seven Principles for Making Marriage Work: A Practical Guide from the Country's Foremost Relationship Expert*. New York: Harmony Books.

Rebuilding Trust and Intimacy

1. Floyd, K. (2006). *Communicating Affection: Interpersonal Behavior and Social Context*. Cambridge: Cambridge University Press.

2. Gulledge, A.K., Gulledge, M.H., & Stahmannn, R.F. (2003). "Romantic physical affection types and relationship satisfaction." *The American Journal of Family Therapy*, 31(4), pp. 233-242.

Leveraging Conflict for Personal and Relational Growth

1. Tedeschi, R.G., & Calhoun, L.G. (2004). Posttraumatic Growth: Conceptual Foundations and Empirical Evidence. Psychological Inquiry, 15(1), pp. 1-18.

2. Gottman, J., & Silver, N. (2015). *The Seven Principles for Making Marriage Work*. New York: Harmony.

3. Kabat-Zinn, J., & Kabat-Zinn, M. (2017). *Everyday Blessings: The Inner Work of Mindful Parenting*. New York: Hyperion.

4. Neff, K. (2011). *Self-Compassion: The Proven Power of Being Kind to Yourself*. New York: William Morrow.

5. Seligman, M.E.P. (2002). *Positive Psychology, Positive Prevention, and Positive Therapy*. In C.R. Snyder & S.J. Lopez (Eds.), *Handbook of Positive Psychology* (pp. 3-12). New York: Oxford University Press.

Inclusive Perspectives on Conflict Resolution

1. Ting-Toomey, S., and Oetzel, J.G. (2013) *Managing Intercultural Conflict Effectively*. Thousand Oaks, CA: Sage Publications.

2. Chen, G.M. (2020) "The Impact of Cultural Awareness on Communication and Conflict Resolution," *Journal of International and Intercultural Communication*, 13(2), pp. 163-178.

3. LeBaron, M. (2003) *Bridging Cultural Conflicts: A New Approach for a Changing World*. San Francisco, CA: Jossey-Bass.

4. Avruch, K. (1998) *Culture and Conflict Resolution*. Washington, DC: United States Institute of Peace Press.

5. Kim, M.S., Lujan, P., and Dixon, L.D. (2008) "Narratives of Nation Building: Constructing a Unified Cultural Identity," *Communication Monographs*, 75(3), pp. 282-304.

6. Gottman, J.M., & Silver, N. (1999) *The Seven Principles for Making Marriage Work*. New York: Crown Publishing Group.

7. Parker, P. (2013) "Navigating the transitions of midlife adult life," *Journal of Marriage and Family Therapy*, 39(3), pp. 232-248.

8. Johnson, S.M. (2008) *Hold Me Tight: Seven Conversations for a Lifetime of Love*. New York: Little, Brown and Company.

9. Gottman, J.M., Levenson, R.W., Gross, J., Frederickson, B.L., McCoy, K., Rosenthal, L., Ruef, A., & Yoshimoto, D. (2010) "The relationship between heart rate reactivity, emotionally supportive behaviors, and relationship satisfaction," *Journal of Family Psychology*, 24(2), pp. 286-295.

10. Meyer, I.H. (2003). "Prejudice, social stress, and mental health in lesbian, gay, and bisexual populations: Conceptual issues and research evidence." *Psychological Bulletin*, 129(5), 674-697.

11. Herek, G.M. (2009). "Hate crimes and stigma-related experiences among sexual minority adults in the United States: Prevalence estimates from a national probability sample." *Journal of Interpersonal Violence*, 24(1), 54-74.

12. Pachankis, J.E. (2014). "Uncovering clinical principles and techniques to address minority stress, mental health, and related health risks among gay and bisexual men." *Clinical Psychology: Science and Practice*, 21(4), 313-330.

13. GLSEN. (2020). *Creating Respectful and Supportive LGBTQ+ Spaces*. [Online] Available at: https://www.glsen.org

14. Wood, J.T., & Dibble, J.L. (2015). *The Dark Side of Relationship Pursuit: From Attraction to Obsession and Stalking*. New York: Routledge.

15. Johnson, S. (2017). *The New Psychology of Love*. Cambridge: Cambridge University Press.

16. Carver, K. (2014). *Emotional Expression and Communication in Relationships*. New York: Harmony Books.

17. Kilmartin, C., & Smiler, A.P. (2015). *The Masculine Self*. New York: Sloan Publishing.

18. Chen, G.M. (2020). "The Impact of Cultural Awareness on Communication and Conflict Resolution," *Journal of International and Intercultural Communication*, 13(2), pp. 163-178.

19. LeBaron, M. (2003). *Bridging Cultural Conflicts: A New Approach for a Changing World*. San Francisco, CA: Jossey-Bass.

20. Ting-Toomey, S., and Oetzel, J.G. (2013). *Managing Intercultural Conflict Effectively*. Thousand Oaks, CA: Sage Publications.

21. Kim, M.S., Lujan, P., and Dixon, L.D. (2008). "Narratives of Nation Building: Constructing a Unified Cultural Identity," *Communication Monographs*, 75(3), pp. 282-304.

Addressing Specific Conflicts

1. Dew, J. (2008). "Two sides of the same coin? The differing roles of assets and consumer debt in marriage." *Journal of Family and Economic Issues*, 29(1), pp. 23-40.

2. Britt, S.L., Huston, S., & Durband, D.B. (2010). "The determinants of money arguments between spouses." *Journal of Financial Therapy*, 1(1), pp. 41-60.

3. Falke, S.I. (2012). "Couples and money: The last taboo." *The American Journal of Family Therapy*, 40(1), pp. 1-19.

4. Archuleta, K.L., Grable, J.E., & Britt, S.L. (2011). "The role of financial therapy in financial planning." *Journal of Financial Planning*, 24(11), pp. 33-42.

5. Cummings, E.M., Merrilees, C.E., & George, M.W. (2014). "Parents' and children's emotions and parenting: Toward an integrated model." *Child Development*, 85(5), pp. 1837-1850.

6. Feinberg, M.E. (2003). "The internal structure and ecological context of coparenting: A framework for research and intervention." *Parenting: Science and Practice*, 3(2), pp. 95-131.

7. McHale, J.P., Lauretti, A., Talbot, J., & Pouquette, C. (2002). "Retrospect and prospect in the psychological study of coparenting and family group process." In M. Bornstein (Ed.), *Handbook of Parenting: Being and Becoming a Parent* (2nd ed., Vol. 3, pp. 127-149). Mahwah, NJ: Lawrence Erlbaum Associates.

8. Simons, R.L., Whitbeck, L.B., Conger, R.D., & Wu, C.-I. (2001). "Intergenerational transmission of harsh parenting." *Developmental Psychology*, 37(1), pp. 840-855.

9. Gottman, J.M., & Silver, N. (1999). *The Seven Principles for Making Marriage Work*. New York: Crown Publishing Group.

10. Johnson, S. (2008). *Hold Me Tight: Seven Conversations for a Lifetime of Love*. New York: Little, Brown and Company.

11. Schnarch, D. (2009). *Intimacy & Desire: Awaken the Passion in Your Relationship*. New York: Beaufort Books.

12. Perel, E. (2017). *The State of Affairs: Rethinking Infidelity*. New York: Harper.

13. Stonebridge, E.A. (2024). *Rekindling Desire: A Couple's Guide to Rediscovering Passion Through Mindfulness and Emotional Connection*. [online] *Amazon*. Independently published. Available at: https://geni.us/89yGV2 [Accessed 5 Mar. 2024].

14. Greenhaus, J.H., & Beutell, N.J. (1985). "Sources of conflict between work and family roles." *Academy of Management Review*, 10(1), pp. 76-88.

15. Kreiner, G.E., Hollensbe, E.C., & Sheep, M.L. (2009). "Balancing borders and bridges: Negotiating the work-home interface via boundary work tactics." *Academy of Management Journal*, 52(4), pp. 704-730.

16. Russo, M., Shteigman, A., & Carmeli, A. (2016). "Workplace and family support and work-life balance: Implications for individual psychological availability and energy at work." *The Journal of Positive Psychology*, 11(2), pp. 173-188.

17. Clark, S.C. (2000). "Work/family border theory: A new theory of work/family balance." *Human Relations*, 53(6), pp. 747-770.

About the author

Evelyn Anne Stonebridge is not just a relationship expert and communication coach; she's a beacon of hope for those navigating the intricate pathways of modern relationships.

With a rich background in psychology and an extensive career in counseling, Evelyn's expertise lies in unraveling the complexities of interpersonal relationships. She seamlessly blends emotional intelligence with effective communication strategies, offering her readers and clients practical yet profoundly insightful guidance. Her work is not just about finding love; it's about nurturing and sustaining it.

As a divorced mother of two wonderful grown-up children, Evelyn's journey into writing began as a new chapter in her life after her children embarked on their adventures. Her experiences as a parent, a partner, and an individual navigating the ups and downs of life infuse her writing with authenticity and heartfelt wisdom.

Now, with a new partner by her side, Evelyn relishes the tranquility of her rural North Carolina home. Here, in the company of her two loyal Irish Setters, she finds the peace and inspiration to continue her work. Her love for long walks in the countryside not only rejuvenates her spirit but also provides a fertile ground for her thoughts and ideas.

Evelyn's approach is not just about solving problems; it's about enriching lives. Her ability to empathize and connect with people from all walks of life makes her a sought-after speaker and consultant. Through her writing and coaching, she continues to touch the lives of many, proving that the power of communication and understanding can indeed transform relationships.

Also by

Explore more works by Evelyn Stonebridge, each offering unique insights and practical guidance to enrich your life and relationships:

The Mindful Relationship Series

- **Harmony in Words: Strengthening Love Through Communication**
  Dive into the art of communication to fortify your love and connection. Available at https://geni.us/HeAW9N

- **Bonds Beyond Time: Mastering the Art of Lifelong Friendships**
  Uncover the secrets to cultivating deep, lasting friendships. Available at https://geni.us/mfEHE57

- **Rekindling Desire: A Couple's Guide to Rediscovering Passion Through Mindfulness and Emotional Connection**
  Rediscover the electrifying connection with your partner. This guide offers practical tools for enhancing communication, reviving intimacy, and reigniting the spark in your relationship. Available at https://geni.us/89yGV2

- **Mindful Moments: A Daily Guide to Mindful Living** (Companion Mindfulness Journal)
  Enhance your daily life with mindfulness through this guided journal, designed to bring peace and awareness to your routine. Available at https://geni.us/auUBsfT

These works collectively offer a comprehensive approach to improving your interpersonal relationships and personal well-being through mindful practices and effective communication.

Printed in Great Britain
by Amazon